W9-CAS-995

ALLEGHENY INTERMEDIATE UNIT
SUNRISE SCHOOL
550 AURA DRIVE
MONROEVILLE, PA 15146

SOON BE FREE

A companion to STEAL AWAY HOME

LOIS RUBY

Aladdin Paperbacks
New York London Toronto Sydney Singapore

First Aladdin Paperbacks edition January 2002
Copyright © 2000 by Lois Ruby
Aladdin Paperbacks
An imprint of Simon & Schuster
Children's Publishing Division
1230 Avenue of the Americas
New York, NY 10020

The Library of Congress has catalogued the hardcover edition as follows:
Ruby, Lois.
Soon be free / Lois Ruby.—1st ed.
p. cm.
Sequel to: Steal away home.
Summary: Thirteen-year-old Dana investigates a mystery involving the old Kansas house that her parents have turned into a bed and breakfast business; in a parallel story, a Quaker boy living in the house in 1857 sets out to help some fugitive slaves to freedom.
ISBN 0-689-83266-4 (hc.)
[1. Fugitive slaves—Fiction. 2. Slavery—Fiction. 3. Underground railroad—Fiction. 4. Quakers—Fiction. 5. Kansas—History—1854-1861—Fiction. 6. Mystery and detective stories.] I. Title.
PZ7.R8314 So 2000   [Fic]—dc21   99-47319
ISBN 0-689-83579-5 (Aladdin pbk.)

*For Jocelyn Charlotte Ruby,
my window to the future*

WE'LL SOON BE FREE

We'll soon be free,
We'll soon be free,
We'll soon be free,
When de Lord will call us home.

My brudder, how long,
My brudder, how long,
My brudder, how long,
'Fore we done sufferin' here?

It won't be long,
It won't be long,
It won't be long,
'Fore de Lord will call us home.

—from an old Negro spiritual

WHAT HAPPENED AND WHEN

There are dozens of names and dates in this story, which takes place both in 1857 and today. Time jumps in the blink of an eye. Maybe this will help.

✳ means an actual historical date; all others are fictional.

1809 Samuel Straightfeather is born.

✳ **1818–1829** By treaty, Delaware Indians are forced out of their homeland in the Delaware Valley ever westward, until they're resettled in Kansas Territory on a reservation of 2 million acres.

✳ **1820** Missouri Compromise allows for Missouri to be admitted to the Union as a slave state and Maine as a free state. Slavery is prohibited from the Louisiana Purchase at the line of 36°30' north latitude, except in the state of Missouri. Thus, slavery is illegal in Kansas Territory.

1822 Jedediah Morrison is born (Bo Prairie Fire's great-great-grandfather).

1844 James Baylor Weaver is born in Boston.

1847 Callie Biggers is born in Kentucky.

✳ **1850** (Second) Fugitive Slave Law is enacted, declaring that runaway slaves must be recaptured and returned to their masters. The new law affirms the principle of *once a slave, always a slave,* reaching back many generations.

✳ **1854** Kansas-Nebraska Act establishes two territories, Kansas and Nebraska, and repeals the Missouri Compromise. Under the doctrine of popular sovereignty, the question of free state or slave state status is left to voters in those states. This act upholds the principle of *once free, always free.*

✳ **1854** Lawrence is founded in Kansas Territory, as is Leavenworth.

✳ **1854** United States treaty with the Delaware Indians reduces the two-million-acre reservation to 275,000 acres, comprising a strip on the north bank of the Kansas River ten miles wide and extending forty miles to the west. This treaty and its repercussions are still being disputed today.

✳ **1856** James Buchanan is elected the fifteenth president of the United States.

1856 Miz Lizbet Charles dies in Lawrence, Kansas Territory.

✴ **1857** After an eleven-year court battle, the Dred Scott decision of the U.S. Supreme Court reaffirms *once a slave, always a slave* and declares that no slave or descendant of a slave can be a U.S. citizen.

1857 Fictional treaty between U.S. and Delaware Indians is signed and lost.

✴ **1858** Gold rush begins in western Kansas Territory, now called Colorado.

1859 Homer Biggers celebrates his fortieth birthday.

✴ **1861** (January 29) Kansas Territory becomes the State of Kansas.

✴ **1861** (April 12) U.S. Civil War / The War Between the States begins.

✴ **1865** (April) Civil War ends when General Lee surrenders.

✴ **1866** Delaware Indians are forced out of Kansas and resettled in Indian Territory (now called Oklahoma), among the Cherokee Nation.

1896 Samuel Straightfeather dies.

1920 Bo Prairie Fire is born.

CONTENTS

SOON BE FREE

Chapter One
FIREBIRD HOUSE

I ask you, why do weird things always happen to me? Mike says it's because blazing redheads are an anomaly of nature, so we're natural magnets for weirdness. He's got a point. Like, not long ago, when we were renovating Firebird House into a bed-and-breakfast, I found a skeleton hidden in a little room upstairs. I followed those bones back into the past and found out that this drafty, creaky old house was once a stop on the Underground Railroad. Not only that, but a runaway slave, Miz Lizbet Charles, had died more than 140 years ago, right here, probably right where I'm sitting this minute.

Mystery solved, right? Hah! Next thing I knew, on a night when there was barely a laser beam of moonlight, a man was snooping around with a flashlight and a shovel in my backyard. It had rained a lot, the yard was a swamp, and the man's boots were ankle-deep in loamy mud.

Now, a normal person would have run for help, but not a blazing redhead. Besides, mud was squishing over my sneakers, so I couldn't have run very fast, anyway, I slogged up behind the man and yelled, "My father's a police captain, you know." Actually, he's a history professor, but this fact wouldn't impress a serious intruder with a shovel and knee-high mud boots.

The man tumbled forward at the sound of my bellow, and the flashlight flew out of his hand and sank into the bog.

He scrambled to regain his balance. His shoulders were no broader than my friend Jeep's, and he had a sort of caved-in look to him, as if he'd had some terrible disease as a child. "I lost my keys," he said, scraping mud off his shirt and pants. They were the high-waisted, plaid kind of pants my uncle Tom used to wear, according to the faded Vietnam-era photos from the seventies.

This man's clown pants were held up with suspenders as wide as chalkboard erasers. Tucked into them was a red flannel shirt buttoned to his chin. You'd think he was ambling in from hoeing the south forty.

"I'm supposed to believe you lost your keys in my yard?"

"Dog ran off with them in his mouth. It's not your business, girl."

"Yes it is, it's my house."

"Wasn't always," he muttered.

"Oh, this is about Miz Lizbet, isn't it?" There'd been lots of publicity since I'd found that skeleton upstairs. All of Lawrence probably all of Kansas—knew how the famous architect James Baylor Weaver had lived in this house when he was a boy, and how his family had harbored runaway slaves until Miz Lizbet died here. "You're looking for something that belonged to her, like you're from a museum or something?"

He took off his glasses and blew on them, polishing them on his shirt. "Now, why would I want some hairpin or button from an old slave, answer me that?"

"Lots of people do, people who are interested in the Underground Railroad."

"I'm not interested."

"Well, then, it's got to be about James Baylor Weaver."

"Never heard of him."

Something in his tone made my blood pump faster, and without his granny glasses, his eyes were hard as bullets. "What *are* you looking for, mister?"

Instead of answering, he sloshed past me and started toward a black Ford parked in front of the house. At first he'd just seemed comical sinking in mud in that weird getup. But then he patted his pockets, and a chill rippled over me when I heard the jingle that told me he hadn't been looking for his keys after all. What did he want in my yard? And had he found what he was looking for?

The old Ford sputtered and cranked, giving me

plenty of time to memorize the Kansas license plate before the man sped away.

Spring rains in Kansas can be fierce. They send earthworms leaping to their death over the side of a culvert. So when I say puddles and mud, you get the picture. Diamonds of light filtered through a lattice wall around the back porch, showing me the man's flashlight beached in the mud with its nose sticking out as if it were gasping for breath. I pulled at it against the resistance of the sludge and swiped the slimy flashlight down my flank. This tells you what an elegant wench I am. *Wench*. Mike's word.

Polished up, the flashlight revealed a plastic stick-on label hanging by a glob of glue:

ERNIE'S BAIT SHOP

Beneath it was an address in Kansas City, Kansas, about forty miles away. Looked like I'd have to figure out a way to drag Mike to Kansas City. Who's this Mike I'm always talking about? Well, he isn't exactly my boyfriend, since he's a full three months younger than I am, and besides, my parents would break out in festering, oozing hives if they thought I had a boyfriend at the tender age of thirteen. Mike's an experiment in progress, still rough like a lump of coal that might just polish up into the Hope Diamond. I'm checking him out carefully as a potential love object when I get to be a freshman, but at this point I can tell you he's no James Baylor Weaver. Sally and Ahn and I, we are all sort of in love with James-at-twelve, even though we know that he grew up and died eighty years before we were even born.

Come to think of it, Mike does have one distinct advantage over James: Mike's still breathing.

Chapter Two
March 1857
A LEG TO STAND ON

Two days before James's thirteenth birthday, the snow finally let up, and he opened the door to a boy with one leg and a crutch that dug inches into the snow because he leaned his weight that way.

"Will Bowers, mercy, what's happened to thee?"

"It's plain cold out here, James Weaver." Will's voice cracked with weariness.

A wave of stinging air sucked James's breath away. "Well, here, let me take thy kit bag."

Will hoisted his weight onto that flimsy crutch and swung himself into the house. James couldn't take his eyes off the leg that wasn't there.

"Got shot," Will said, lowering himself onto the bench at the kitchen table. A pinned-up trouser leg hung like a sack below the bench. Dried blood had turned it the color of an ax left to rust in the rain. Will eyed a plate covered with one of Ma's embroidered flour-sack tea towels.

James offered him a biscuit that was no better than hardtack, but Will swallowed it in two bites without even a smear of butter or apple jelly. He ate right through the rest of the biscuits like he hadn't had supper, or dinner before that.

"Surgeon sawed it off."

James's stomach lurched. He kept hearing Grandpa Baylor's voice: "I tell you, boy, a man doesn't have a leg to stand on unless he's honest to the bone," and now Grandpa Baylor was gone and Ma was on her way back from burying him in Boston, and here Will Bowers hadn't but one leg to stand on.

"It was the Border Ruffians did it." Will dabbed at every crumb on the table until he had a good supply to suck off his finger.

"At least thee's alive," James said, although he wondered if he'd want to be alive with only one leg. What did it look like inside that sack? Was it as raw as fresh meat, or had it healed over into ropy scars?

"Funny thing is, I still feel it."

"Feel what, Will?"

"A whole leg. There's a blister on my heel from a wet boot. Itches on the bottom of my foot, too."

It was too gruesome to think about, so James said, "Ma's been gone to Boston to bury my grandfather. She and my sister have been gone three months. Pa and I thought they'd be back by Christmas, but here it is the first of March. Until the last day or two, the snow's been too deep for travel cross-country. Doesn't stop my pa, though. He's over in Topeka on Kansas Territory business."

"Some things never change."

"Oh, Will, I'm mighty sorry about thy leg."

Will petted the stump as if it were a dog nipping at him under the table. "Guess I'm lucky. Didn't I stand right there at your door last September and say I might come back in a box?"

"Thee did. Thee caused quite a stir in my house." James chuckled. "I'd have gone with thee, but it's not the Quaker way. My ma and pa would have had fits."

Will filled his palm with salt from the little salt-cellar and licked his hand clean.

"Thee's starving." James jumped up and brought Will back some jerky and a cup of cold tea.

"What would you have done over there at Pottawatomie with John Brown's posse, James?" Will chewed away on that dried meat strip. "Talked to them pretty with all your thees and thous? That would have turned two or three dozen proslavers back and made them kneel and say their prayers right out loud."

James felt his scalp prickle, coward that he was. Here they were, living right on the edge of Kansas Territory, which was free, and Missouri, which was a slave state. Border skirmishes were raging all around them. Every Lawrence man had taken up arms, except Dr. Olney and Pa and half a dozen other men in town who were Quakers. Mercy, even one of the Quakers was keeping a rifle clean and greased, just in case.

Flaring with anger—or was it shame?—James asked, "Why's thee here instead of at thy own place?"

"It's four more blocks. Try walking halfway across Kansas on a crutch."

"There's another reason."

"Which is?"

"Only thee knows. But I suspect it has something to do with being afraid to go home."

"I'm not afraid of anything. I've followed John Brown into a raid on a camp of Border Ruffians. Sliced one up myself. I watched that doctor take off my leg with just a shot of whiskey to dull the ache."

James shuddered. "There's a draft in here."

"Heck, I'm not afraid of anything," Will said again. "Except my ma. She'll fall over dead when she sees me like this. Reckon I can stay here tonight? I can face Ma better when the sun's just coming up."

James glanced at the spot in front of the fire where the cat, Trembles, raced her motor. Weeks ago Solomon, who was a free Negro, had lain on a pallet by that fire, sweating through his typhoid fever while Miz Lizbet had nursed him back to health.

Miz Lizbet. What a vexing woman she was, but how James missed her! Six weeks had passed since she'd died in this house.

Then Will startled him with a question: "Still harboring runaway slaves?"

"Thee knew?"

"Everybody in town knew, except your pa."

"Naw, not anymore, we're not."

"So, you letting me stay here tonight like those runaways did? Least I'm not against any law."

"We could make thee up a pallet on the floor by the fire. Thee wouldn't have to manage stairs."

Will nodded. "I swear, I could sleep a week."

And he nearly did. He slept around the clock until Ma and Rebecca came back after being gone to Boston for three long months and found a one-legged boy asleep in the parlor.

Chapter Three
SKELETON KEY

I told the kids in the lunchroom on Monday, "There was this really weird guy hanging around in my yard last night with a shovel and a flashlight."

"What did he want?" Mike tilted his head back, and a sheet of straight black hair hung over his collar as he let a canned peach slice slither down his throat like a raw oyster. He has some amusing mannerisms, if you're into zoological feeding customs.

"That is so revolting." Sally wrinkled her freckled nose. "What was the guy, a gas-meter reader?"

Jeep popped the last of his sandwich into his mouth, and his words came out peanut-butter garbled. "On a Sunday night? With a shovel and a flashlight?"

"He said he was looking for his car keys."

"Oh, yeah, I'd buy that," Jeep said.

I held a spoonful of Swiss Miss tapioca in front of my lips. I know Mike hates tapioca because it reminds him of why he goes to the dermatologist.

"How can you eat stuff that looks like zits?" he asked.

"Like this." I slid the spoon into my mouth and

slurgged the pudding off. "Delicious." The Cafeteria Werewolf came by and snapped up two of those vomit-colored trays. I smiled at her, which always makes the fur stand up on her arms. I said, "Whatever the guy was looking for out there, I'm sure it had to do with James."

"We gotta bring *him* into the picture again?" Mike protested. "The guy's been dead since before man started walking upright, and you women talk about him like he's a box office sensation." He flicked his tongue over his braces. There didn't seem to be enough room in his mouth for both his tongue and all that hardware. I know, I'm making him sound grotesque. He's actually kind of cute with those dimples that drill his cheeks when he laughs. And he laughs a lot.

Sally, all business, said, "Okay, guys, let's think this through. What's the working theory?"

"None, yet," I admitted. "Ahn, what do you think?"

Ahn was eating Asian foods she'd brought from home, things that looked like stringy spinach and crunchy Styrofoam strips. "Unknown at this time."

"Wait and see if the creep turns up again," Jeep suggested. I loved the glow of his newly shaved brown head, oiled and glistening in the harsh cafeteria lights. Jeep is a young Michael Jordan, only it will probably be two years before he is eye level with MJ's belt buckle.

12

The noise in the cafeteria was becoming a thundering roar. "Five minutes till we go down to the Dungeon," Mike shouted over the chaos. The basement of Thoreau Middle School is as indestructible as a Roman fortress. We have science down there just in case a chemical experiment explodes or one of the reptiles gets loose, which is something we engineer pretty regularly. We are eighth graders. We are *supposed* to do stuff like that.

The cafeteria was starting to clear out, and it sounded like a train rumbling through a subway station. I yelled, "Did I mention I got the man's flashlight?" Mike raised an eyebrow in interest.

"With his address on it. Anyone want to go to Kansas City?"

"How?" Mike asked.

"We could hitchhike," Jeep said, tossing his fork and knife into a tub of soapy water. *Splat*. The Cafeteria Werewolf wiped her cheeks with her paws and scowled at Jeep. We were dying to catch her some night howling at the full moon.

"Hitchhike and risk certain death," Sally reminded him.

"You afraid of a little old psychopathic truck driver, Sal?" Mike asked.

"No, my parents, if they found out."

"Don't worry, we'll get a ride," I assured them all.

Mike smashed the last of his peaches with his

13

milk carton. "We're infants; we're driver's licensely challenged, remember?"

"You always see the glass half empty. I'm conceiving a plan, Mike."

He groaned. "A Dana plan. We're all doomed."

That weekend we had the grand opening of Firebird House, named that because it had risen from the ashes of one fire plus both sackings of Lawrence. Now it was starting its fourth lifetime. Our own Firebird, a turquoise-and-yellow parakeet, watched with great boredom as we hung a rustic wooden placard on the wall next to his cage:

HOME OF ARCHITECT
JAMES BAYLOR WEAVER (1844–1906)
AND OF ELIZABETH CHARLES,
BORN IN SLAVERY AROUND 1832
AND LAID TO REST IN THIS HOUSE IN 1856

We peeked from behind the new pink window sheers as the first customers pulled up in a car that seemed familiar. When Mom led them upstairs, I studied the register where Mr. and Mrs. Raymond Berk had scrawled their names and their Overland Park address, and the license plate number of their car.

It was the same old Ford that the man from Ernie's Bait Shop had driven.

Now I was more than curious; I *had* to find out

what they were looking for, especially if it had something to do with James Weaver.

The old-fashioned Victorian doors at Firebird House have the kind of keyholes big enough to see through, but that wouldn't have been enough to satisfy me.

I had a skeleton key; all I had to do was wait for the Berks to get hungry.

Chapter Four
March 1857
WILL IN THE SHADOWS

Will seemed to want to make himself scarce for James's reunion with his mother and sister, so he hung back in the shadow of the keeping room.

James was itching to throw his arms around Ma; three long months she'd been gone. Three months' worth of barely passable meals, and every shirt gray as dishwater, begging for her scrub board, and every pair of britches sorely wanting Ma's swift needle.

But with Will hulking around there in the shadows, James didn't dare whoop at Ma. Instead, he picked up his little sister, Rebecca, and whirled her around the room. "Thee's grown a yard!" he said happily. "Thee weighs pretty nearly a ton."

Ma beamed at James. "What is that caterpillar that's crawled up under thy nose, James?"

James slapped his hand to the coppery fuzz above his lip and jerked his head toward the corner. "Say hello to Will, Ma."

"Will Bowers, why on earth is thee hiding in the corner like a mouse?" James watched Ma's eyes pass over Will. She sized up the situation with barely a glance. She turned her attention to housekeeping, running her finger through a winter's worth of dust on the hutch. "Thee's lacked a woman's touch," Ma said, holding up the coffee kettle with the hole James had burned clear through it.

"Yes, ma'am," James said shyly.

Rebecca darted and spun, inspecting every inch of the room. "Grandma Baylor's house in Boston is so much prettier," she said mournfully, "but here's where my toys are." She opened the wicker basket where her rag babies and rubber balls and spinning tops were heaped.

Ma said, "Run upstairs and see about stripping sheets off thy bed. I suspect James hasn't done the laundry in a month of Mondays." She gave Will a good, hard look and flinched just a bit as she came to the empty leg sack. Eyeing the rumpled pallet on the floor, she said, "Will Bowers, thee must get on home. The snow's nearly melted, and thy mother must be frantic with worry for thee."

"Yes, Mrs. Weaver."

"Thee mustn't fret. She's a strong woman," Ma said gently. She gathered Will's bag and handed him his crutch. "Go home, Will Bowers. God bless."

Once the door was shut behind him, Ma raced toward James. "Oh, son," she cried. "Thee's just about the finest sight I've seen in weeks." She pulled James to her, sniffing his fiery hair that wanted a good washing "It's thy birthday, James. I'd have fought Bengal tigers to make it home in time. Where's thy father?"

"Be home by nightfall, Ma."

"Oh, I have missed thee both so much, my teeth have fairly ached for thee. And Miss Elizabeth, James? Where is she this day?"

"Gone," James said.

"Back to Kentucky again?" Ma asked softly. He was sure she sensed what he was about to tell her. How would Ma ever forgive them?

Palms sweating, he said, "Typhoid fever took her from us, Ma. Miz Lizbet's dead."

Chapter Five
WALKING ON EGG YOLKS

I jogged over to Ahn's house on Vermont. It's a ramshackle bungalow that she shares with a flock of brothers and cousins who've come from Vietnam, without parents, all at different times. Ahn is the main cook for the family since she's the only one who doesn't have a job, as if round-the-clock short-order cook isn't a job.

About six people were studying all over the floor in the front room when I burst into the house. "Where's Ahn?"

One brother—I can never remember which is which, because they all seem to be the same age—called to Ahn in Vietnamese, and she came out of the kitchen with a spatula in her hand.

"Ahn, remember I told you about Ernie, the bait shop man, who invaded my yard?"

The scholarly types all glared at me, so I lowered my voice. "Well, he's sent two other spies, the Berks, in the same car, and they made sure to check in the first day we were open, before there were any other guests. I just know they're looking for something major."

"Maybe you're too suspicious," Ahn whispered,

wiping the spatula on her apron. She slid out the door and closed it without a sound. "Nho has his Ph.D. comprehensive exams next week. He's a little tense," she explained. "We are all walking on egg yolks."

"Shells. Anyway, here's a chance for you to get away. It's Friday. Come spend the night at my house and we'll keep an eye on the Berks."

Ahn looked worried. "I must give Nho a good breakfast tomorrow. He needs fuel for his study engine."

"Come over and I'll fix a cheese omelette as big as a pizza. You can take it back to him in the morning."

Food is always scarce at Ahn's, so she was won over. "With tomatoes¿ Green peppers¿ Onions¿ Nho will be in heaven."

That night we sipped hot, spiced cider from University of Kansas Jayhawk mugs and waited in the parlor for the Berks to come back from dinner. As soon as the bell tinkled over the front door, I jumped up. "Welcome back to Firebird House," I sang as Mr. and Mrs. Berk started for the stairs. "Why not come into the parlor¿ My dad's got a fire going. These old houses stay cold as a tomb until July."

"I'm going to bed," Mr. Berk grumbled, and he ran up the stairs as if he might not make it to the bathroom in time. Mrs. Berk came into the parlor, rattling trinkets on the tables in her wake. She pushed up the raglan sleeves of her huge magenta sweater and settled into a brocade love seat that was all out of proportion for her. She was like a hippo on a bar stool.

Her eyes roved over every inch of the room. "Old houses like this bury their secrets," she said. Her mean eyes settled on mine, and a shiver worked its way up my back like cold puppy paws. I remembered something Grammy Shannon used to say: "It was like a ghost walked over my grave."

What was Mattie Berk up to?

NO MORE TALK OF A DEAD BODY

"Miss Elizabeth dead? Oh, mercy." Ma stood in front of the fire, drying the hem of her skirt, and for a few heavy seconds the only sound in the room was the *whoosh-whoosh* of the gray worsted fabric at her heels. James knew Ma was praying, in the silent way Quakers do.

When she turned to him, her face was twisted with grief. "Thy father?"

"A blizzard kept him away. Then he came home one day and found Miz Lizbet here."

"He never wrote to tell me this. Curious."

"Pa's forgiven thee for hiding the runaways and for lying to him."

"Well, I believe he knew I had the Negroes here, anyway, but he never let on. Did he give Miss Elizabeth a proper Christian burial?"

Before James could answer, Rebecca came down the stairs, dragging linen like a dingy bridal train. "Ma, that little room we built so no one could hear James's screechy violin playing? It's gone."

Ma turned her eyes on James. "Thee's built a wall?"

And then he poured the whole story like milk from a pitcher. "Marshal Fain was onto us, Ma, just laying a trap. He posted his men outside, round the clock. Snow was up to our windows, and they kept clearing it off so they could see in. They were set on catching us in the act of hiding those runaways."

"Thee must have been scared to death," Rebecca said. "I'd have been."

"Thee's six. Pa and Solomon and I are men," James replied gruffly.

"Solomon was here, too?" asked Ma.

"Yes, ma'am. He had the typhoid fever first, and Miz Lizbet nursed him through. This was before Marshal Fain's men took up outside our door. Miz Lizbet slept beside him right there in front of the fire." James nodded toward Will's pallet. "Washed him night and day, like you did Rebecca when she was burning up with fever. By the time his fever broke, she was sick herself. About then's when Marshal Fain's men planted themselves out there. So we moved Miz Lizbet upstairs to the screechy violin room, and Solomon tended her night and day like she'd done him."

"They were sweet on each other," Ma said, then caught herself. "Still, it wasn't proper, a lady and a gentleman."

"They meant to marry as soon as Miz Lizbet got well, but she didn't."

Rebecca's eyes were dark and wide as sunflower centers. "Did Miz Lizbet die, James?"

Ma reached out and took Rebecca under her wing. "Brave soul, she's gone to her reward. James, the burial?"

"I'm coming to that." How was he to tell Ma that forever they'd be living in a house with a dead body?

Ma said, "Well, now, thee couldn't take her outside, what with the marshal's men watching thy every move. And the ground was too frozen to dig a proper grave." Ma's voice got hard as gravel. "What did thy father do with poor Miss Elizabeth, James?"

"He said what needed to be said at her funeral service, commending her to the Lord and all."

"And then?" Ma asked impatiently.

James bristled. "Well, what choice did we have, Ma? If the marshal had gotten Miz Lizbet alive, he'd have hauled her back to her owner in Kentucky."

"One person does not *own* another, James."

"It's the law, at least the way they read it. But if he'd gotten her dead, there's no telling what those Border Ruffians would have done to her body." James felt tears pounding the backs of his eyes. He mustn't cry like a baby on his thirteenth birthday. He was sure Will hadn't cried over that leg of his.

Then Rebecca saved him having to say the words that would hurt the most. "Why, thee must have left her upstairs and walled her off!"

Ma clapped her hand to her mouth. "James, she lies upstairs?"

24

"Yes, ma'am," he whispered.

Rebecca stamped her foot, and the floorboards buckled. "James, how could thee? Oh, poor Miz Lizbet, all dead and alone like that."

Ma's lips moved in prayer, as if she were reading. After the longest time, she said, "Thee did the honorable thing, James Baylor Weaver, thee and thy father and Solomon."

Rebecca wrinkled her nose. "Why, how she must have smelled!"

James nodded, remembering those horrid first weeks.

"Remember last summer when Jilly died having her pups, and we didn't find the poor things for a week? Remember, Ma? Thee gave me a handkerchief soaked in rosewater to put to my nose, but I can still smell Jilly." She sniffed the air. "I believe I smell Miz Lizbet, too."

Ma cast Rebecca a stern scowl and said, "There will be no more talk of a dead body in this house."

"Yes, Ma," Rebecca said with a groan.

"James? No more talk. Does thee hear me?"

"Clear as a whippoorwill, Ma."

Ma took a deep breath. "Now, has thee anything left in the pantry that I might turn into a decent meal? Thee must be hungry, James. Thee's thin as a carrot."

"There hasn't been one good meal since thee left," James admitted.

"Fire the oven, son," Ma ordered. "What's a birthday without a cake?" She pulled down the canister of flour and picked out tiny black bugs that had mercifully died with the winter freeze.

Chapter Seven
TOO MUCH HISTORY

Silvery-cold air hissed through the uneven joints of the windows behind us. Firebird fluttered his yellow wings to rustle up a little warmth. I could swear he said, "Brrrr!"

Mattie Berk pulled her sweater over her hands and muttered, "You call this spring?"

"The house is nearly one hundred fifty years old," I reminded her. We all three drifted over to the fireplace and toasted our hands.

Ahn, who knows the history of Firebird House as well as I do, began the saga.

"It was built the first time in 1855, then again in 1856, after a fire. In 1863 the kitchen was destroyed in William Quantrill's raid, but the upper floor was safe."

"Yeah, yeah, including the room with the skeleton."

"Not just a skeleton, Mrs. Berk," Ahn said indignantly. "It was Miz Lizbet Charles. She died of typhoid fever in that room. Her sweetheart, Solomon, took care of her until he closed her eyes for the last time."

"Sad tale." Mrs. Berk ran her hand around a section of wainscoting. "Is this the original wood?"

"All of it," I boasted. "My mom and I stripped it and refinished every inch of it."

I watched the woman closely. She was inspecting the wall as if she might find a trapdoor or a bogus bookcase that swung open into a secret room. Maybe she knew something I didn't.

She tapped the floor with her foot, which was about the size of a Ping-Pong paddle. "Floor seems solid. Ever have to pull up the floorboards?" She wore hefty shoulder pads and had no waist. All that bulk stood on two thick piano legs. She sank back into the love seat and sent it rocking on its back legs. "Talk to me about the Weaver family."

Obviously she already knew a lot about the Weavers, but I volunteered, "They were Quakers, agents on the Underground Railroad."

"Mrs. Weaver was, not Mr.," Ahn explained. "He didn't approve of hiding slaves, but he was an abolitionist, too—"

Mrs. Berk interrupted her. "Talk to me about James."

Ahn picked up a photo of Wolcott Castle, taken at its rededication the previous summer. "James Weaver designed this beautiful house where forty people could live and never run out of hot water."

Mrs. Berk glanced at the picture. I could tell it wasn't the first time she'd seen it. "He was some famous architect, I've heard."

"Oh, yes," Ahn agreed, "but he was only twelve when we knew him."

"What are you talking about? The guy lived in the last century."

"Of course," Ahn said gently. "But we knew him well."

"Whatever." Mrs. Berk wasn't big on romance. But she sure was nosy. "I heard something about a diary you found upstairs. Anything good in it?"

"Of course!" Ahn said, insulted. "It was all about Mrs. Weaver and Miz Lizbet and the people running away, the slaves. *Very* good."

"Yeah, yeah, but anything about Weaver's buildings?"

"No," I answered. "Mrs. Weaver's diary was written way before James started designing buildings." I thought of his redheaded self at my age, spending long evenings without TV or video games, sketching houses and barns and churches by candlelight. Imagine what he could have done with a Macintosh!

Mrs. Berk lit up a cigarette, striking the match on the rough wood sign with Smokey Bear saying, THANKS FOR NOT SMOKING, FOLKS! She tossed the lit match into the fireplace. Ahn rushed forward with her cider mug as an ashtray.

Mrs. Berk said, "Find any of Weaver's architectural drawings stashed away in this house?"

I shook my head. "I guess they'd be valuable if we had."

"Valuable?" Mrs. Berk shrugged her mighty shoulders and exhaled a cloud of stinky smoke. "No, not especially."

Ahn and I glanced at each other while Mrs. Berk picked lint off her broad-beam navy blue slacks. "Well, I'm turning in. The fire's making me groggy. Too much history, I guess. You're not light sleepers, are you? Raymond and I keep the radio on low all night."

"No problem," Ahn said. "Dana's family sleeps like a brick."

"A *log*, Ahn."

Mrs. Berk faked a wide yawn. She pulled her thick knees together and stood up. Whatnots rattled again. "Catch you in the morning."

When her wide rear end was halfway up the stairs, I whispered, "Not if we catch you first." *And we will catch her*, I thought. Somehow I'd find out what the Berks knew about James Weaver, who'd scratched out awful violin tunes and sketched his first buildings within these walls—and buried Miz Lizbet behind one of them.

I'd read a description of James Weaver in his mother's diary. He and I shared the same copper-wire hair and blue green eyes, the same paper-pale skin, as if we were twins who, through a weird accident of birth, were separated by fifteen decades. If anyone was going to learn something new about James, it was going to be me, not Mattie Berk.

Chapter Eight
March 1857
COCKLEBURS

Pa and James washed up out back. Pa had layers of travel dirt to scrub away before Ma would let him offer the blessing for supper. After supper, James would tend to Buttermilk, who'd carried Pa all those miles. Buttermilk's chestnut coat was matted with sweat, and the white mottled zigzag that gave her her name looked gray as wash water.

"Long trip," James said. He was always shy for words when he was alone with Pa. With Ma around, conversation flowed more easily, and of course, Rebecca never stopped yammering for a second.

"I'd have run Buttermilk like a racehorse if I'd known thy ma would be waiting home."

"Lucky for Buttermilk thee didn't know." The horse flicked the first of the season's flies off with her tail.

Pa's eyes darted up toward the point just under the roof of their house. "Thee got it all settled, the business over Miss Elizabeth?" His voice was tight. Why, he was afraid of Ma!

"Yes, sir, she knows, and she knows thee knows, and she says there'll be no more talk of dead bodies in the house."

Pa nodded, relieved.

"I suspect she'll have a few more thoughts on the subject when she gets thee alone," James said, snickering.

"Now that thee's thirteen, thee's an authority on women?"

"Just Ma," James replied quickly. He wiped his hands on an old flannel blanket flung over the stockade fence. Bethany Maxwell came across his mind, as she did all too often. She was as beautiful as a newborn piglet—and just as slippery. She'd gone off to California with her family and hadn't sent back a single word. But he had Trembles, her Siamese, to remind him of Bethany's blue eyes.

"Well," Pa said, rolling his sleeves back down. He buttoned them between his pale wrists and large, windburned hands. "I for one am glad to have the whole episode with the runaways behind me."

"Thee has cockleburs behind thee also," James said.

Pa patted his rear. "Ouch!" He picked them off, dusting off his trousers, and he straightened his shirt and turned his hat just so. "Reckon thy mother will find me presentable?"

"Yes, sir." James thought his father admirably handsome—tall and broad and full-bearded. James, with his red hair and freckled, milky skin, would grow up to look nothing like Pa. He'd look more like Grandpa Baylor, and it saddened him to remember that he'd never again share his thoughts with Grandpa Baylor.

Growing up, he thought, *you sure lose a lot of people you'd rather have around a bit longer.*

Chapter Nine
CAUGHT!

The radio in the Berks' room hummed with some all-night talk show, and Mr. and Mrs. Berk talked right over it.

"How much could they possibly have to say to each other? No one in my family talks this much," Ahn said, with a jelly jar to the wall. "Can you make out anything?"

"It sounds like an argument to me." I yanked my Thoreau Middle School nightshirt over my knees. It was already stretched enough to fit a sumo wrestler.

"You listen for a while." Ahn handed me the jar and dropped onto the twin bed. The bed springs squealed.

"Shh! They're not supposed to know we're still awake."

"I'm not." Soon Ahn was snoring gently.

I blew an errant red curl off my forehead and read Henry David Thoreau's words spread across the hump of my knees: *"To be awake is to be alive."* And under that, bold red letters said, *"I went to the woods because I wished to live deliberately. . . ."* Was I the only one with any sense of adventure?

I lay in the dark, *deliberately* waiting for—what?

Wait! The Berks' door opened with a snick. There was a light footstep in the carpeting. It had to be Mr. Berk, because Mrs. Berk would be bending floorboards. A shadow darkened the slit of hall light under my door. He stood right outside my room, not moving an inch. Listening, no doubt, to make sure I was asleep.

I joined Ahn's breathing rhythm. Together we sounded like a sinus infection. The shadow slid away, and the strip of light returned. Where was he going?

"Ahn, wake up," I whispered. "Mr. Berk's roaming out there." Ahn flopped over on her stomach and pulled the pillow over her head.

I spread out on the floor with my ear to the narrow lath of light. I heard Firebird's nightly protest— "Squawk! Squawk! Brrrrook!"—as Dad tossed the sheet over the cage to silence the beast for the night. Mom and Dad came upstairs, their footsteps like drumbeats. They closed the door to their room, and in a minute I heard the TV up loud, no doubt to drown out the Berks' radio.

I opened my door a crack. Now Mr. Berk was stepping into the winter wardrobe closet. It's a walk-in, but only tall enough for a dwarf. He dropped to his knees and pulled the closet door shut behind him.

I tiptoed down the hall until I was just outside the closet. From inside came a *tap-tap-tap,* as if a woodpecker were working his way along the wall. Suddenly I noticed a strip of light under the bathroom door. Mrs. Berk must be in there! When had she left her room without my hearing?

I dashed back and hid behind my bedroom door until my heart stopped pounding and I couldn't resist cracking the door open again.

There was a *yeowl* from inside the hall closet, muffled by the winter coats. Grateful for the amber night-light in the hall, I watched as Mrs. Berk opened the bathroom door. "Raymond?" she whispered. Mr. Berk was hopping around like a man who'd been walking barefoot over hot coals. "Raymond, what's that thing?" asked Mrs. Berk.

Mr. Berk shook his foot around. A mousetrap dangled from his big toe. "Get it off!"

Mrs. Berk straddled his leg as if she were shoeing a horse and fiddled with the spring. "Ignoramus!" she hissed.

"It hurts, Mattie! Where's your motherly compassion?"

"I'm not your mother. Hold still, I've almost got it. It's not going to help if the whole thing snaps shut on my finger. Hold still, Raymond. There."

Mr. Berk sat on the floor and lifted his toe to his face. "It's already black and blue. I'll probably lose the nail." He popped the toe into his mouth and rocked himself.

"Oh, Raymond, really. Well, it's obvious we're not going to find anything tonight while you're suffering such toe agonies." She led him roughly by the collar of his robe. He limped more than he needed to until they disappeared behind their door. The radio was snapped off.

I held the jelly jar to the wall until I heard rhythmic breathing. Tomorrow, while they were out, I'd search their room. It was only fair; hadn't Mr. Berk searched our hall closet? The difference was, *he* knew what he was looking for; I'd have to fly blind.

Chapter Ten
March 1857
MIZ LIZBET'S LEGACY

"Amen," Pa said, and Ma began dishing out supper: hard-cooked eggs that she'd preserved in limewater before she went east; green beans and wild raspberries she'd put up last summer; and biscuits that stood two inches high and soaked up butter like the dry earth swallowed rain.

Rebecca sat on Pa's knee, even eating from his plate. This wasn't something Ma approved of, but after three months' absence, she'd let up on them a bit. "Pa, did thee know Miz Lizbet's upstairs turning ashes to ashes, dust to dust?"

Ma tapped Rebecca's hand with a fork. "I remind thee, there's to be no talk of dead bodies."

"Yes, ma'am," Rebecca said, as though all the fun had been yanked from her evening.

"That doesn't prevent us from talking about live ones," Ma said. "I refer to the ones who wait for Miss Elizabeth in Kentucky."

James put a rubbery bite of egg in his mouth, dreading what she'd say next.

"Thee knows, each of thee, that Miss Elizabeth's work is not done."

Pa's beard was greasy with hot butter. "Yes, Millicent, she told us of the slaves prepared to run away. However, Mrs. Weaver, it appears they shall have to wait for another shepherd."

"Precisely, Mr. Weaver." Ma dangled a green bean from her fork, lost in thought.

She's hatching, James told himself. *Mercy.* Also, it meant trouble when his parents called each other mister and missus.

Pa moved Rebecca off his knee. "Thy mother has a plan," he muttered, and James groaned.

"Tell it, Ma! Is it exciting? Will there be more dead bodies upstairs?" Rebecca squirmed on the bench beside Pa.

Ma laid the green bean down on her plate. "It is up to us to finish her work. James, has thee an idea?"

"No, ma'am." He held his breath. She had one, no doubt.

"Thee gentlemen must go to Kentucky and rescue those brave Negroes." Ma kept her eyes aimed at her plate, but James caught her studying him out of the corner of one eye.

Pa wiped his beard and slammed his napkin down on the table. "Unthinkable, Mrs. Weaver. As a lawyer, I'm an officer of the court, and a representative of the Kansas Territory government. I'm sworn to uphold the law. Need I remind thee that it's illegal to aid and abet runaway slaves? Look how I've compromised my position already, allowing that woman to live in this house."

"And die in this house," Ma reminded him.

Rebecca's imitation of Ma's voice was perfect: "There's to be no more talk of dead bodies in this house."

Ma smiled, so Pa smiled, and James took advantage of this opportunity to shovel in two more eggs and a biscuit. The green beans could turn gray and moldy for all he cared, but those sweet, tangy raspberries . . .

"Solomon Jefferson will go after them," Ma said.

"It's risky, Mrs. Weaver, even with papers proving he's a free man. Thee recalls how he was taken off by a slave catcher just last year?"

"And returned, due to thy conscientious legal work," Ma said, giving Pa this small peace offering. Boy, did she ever know how to butter him up! "Yes, Solomon will have to go."

James watched a flush of anger rise up Pa's neck. "Millicent, thee's been in Boston all winter. Thee's thinking like a Yankee. But we are living in Kansas Territory, where ruffians do not always heed the law of the land."

"Law, piffle," Ma said. "Does thee not recognize a higher law? Does thee not hear a still, silent voice beyond thy own, Mr. Weaver?"

"No, I do not, Mrs. Weaver."

Ma tucked a towel around the two biscuits James wished were his own. Her graceful fingers lingered over the basket, a wire-thin gold ring their only adornment. James and Rebecca looked down at their plates while the angry words hung in the air. Finally Ma said, "Then thee must be silent, Caleb, to let the voice into thy head."

Silence, James thought, *Quaker silence. Their blessing and their curse.*

After a long while, Ma said, "So, we're agreed? Solomon Jefferson will go after those blessed souls waiting in Kentucky?"

Pa nodded, working his tongue round inside his cheeks. James could see he was stewing.

"And thee, James, must go along with Solomon," Ma continued.

"Me? Ma!"

Pa's words were clipped: "Mrs. Weaver, I implore thee to consider the boy's welfare, as well as the law of the land."

"Mr. Weaver, *thee* must lift thy nose from thy law books now and again." She squared her shoulders and turned back to James. "Well, now, is thee to hide behind thy little boy britches? Thee's thirteen today."

A vein throbbed in Pa's temple as he pushed the food around on his plate. He opened his mouth, but Ma spoke first.

"I've baked a birthday cake for thee, James. We'll each have a generous wedge."

Rebecca complained, "It's a honey cake with walnuts, even though thee all know I hate walnuts."

"Then thy slice shall go to Solomon," Ma snapped.

James mashed green beans into a pulp and kept one eye on Pa, who sat at the table's head, with his fingers locked over his lips and his eyes blazing. Surely Pa would save him from the awful venture. Why was *he* to be sent to guide the runaways North? He had only a sketchy idea of where Kentucky was and very little common sense. All he wanted to do was draw buildings. Buildings that flowed into the earth they grew out of, buildings framed by the blue horizon, buildings that twinkled in the black of night with lamps carefully spaced in all the windows.

Ma had lit a thick, white candle in the middle of the cake. "Happy birthday, son." Her mouth was soft, and her eyes glistened in the candlelight. "Caleb, make way." Pa drew back on the bench, averting his eyes as Ma set the flaming cake down in front of James. "Tonight we celebrate awhile, before we plan thy journey."

James let out a sigh, and the puff of air made the candle flicker just before Rebecca blew it out, as if it were *her* birthday and not his.

Pa left the table, to see about the horse, Buttermilk, he said. But James knew Pa was still mad at Ma. It wasn't the homecoming, it wasn't the birthday he'd been hoping for.

Chapter Eleven
TRAP

The next morning we propped the swinging door open from the kitchen to check out the scene in the dining room. The Berks were gobbling half a sour cream coffee cake and a quart of giant strawberries dipped in powdered sugar. Mr. Berk guzzled freshly squeezed orange juice as if it were tap water. Mom hovered over them, pouring juice and coffee just about every time they swallowed.

Behind me, the butter began to sizzle on the stove. Ahn chopped onions and peppers and tomatoes while I beat the eggs and poured them into the skillet. When they started growing a brown crust around the edges, I added Ahn's veggies and a handful of cheddar shavings. The omelette was a cholesterol nightmare, but Ahn's brother wouldn't mind.

From the dining room, Mom was trying to be civil as the Berks ate everything except the jonquils at the center of the table. "So, what's on your agenda for today, folks?"

Mrs. Berk said, "We're off to the Watkins Museum to do a little research."

43

"Are you writing a book?" Her question was make-talk, but Mr. Berk got fired up.

"You're new at this bed-and-breakfast thing, aren't you? *Rulo numero uno:* Don't put your guests through the third degree."

"Raymond," Mrs. Berk warned.

Mom sounded bright and cheerful, but I heard the bark in her voice, and knew it was only a matter of time until the Mistress of Sarcasm struck. "You might consider visiting Wolcott Castle. It was designed by our own James Baylor Weaver, you know."

Mr. Berk said, "That so?"

"As if he didn't know," I whispered to Ahn.

"Well," Mom said too brightly, "have a great day. There's a lovely Mexican hacienda restaurant over on Mass if you like hand-rolled tamales."

Their chairs scraped against the hardwood floor as they started for the stairs.

"You have a bit of a limp this morning, Mr. Berk." Mom couldn't have known about the mouse-trap, could she? Yet her words were sharp and pointed, piercing like darts. "Did you have an accident? Or is it rheumatism?"

"New shoes," he grumbled.

"Nice joint you got here," Mattie said, to take the heat off her husband. "Plenty old-time charm."

Mom said, "Yes, but you know these old houses. Sometimes you get a mouse or two. The house has been in their family for a hundred generations, and they think they've got squatters' rights. I guess we ought to have a cat roaming the halls. That way we'd never have to set out a mousetrap, would we?"

Mr. Berk sprayed a mouthful of orange juice across the table.

Chapter Twelve
March 1857
DRED SCOTT

James stacked the last of the supper dishes on the hutch, while Pa held a boot between his knees and polished it so long and hard that James thought he'd swipe the leather clean off.

James lined up all the forks and knives in the drawer just the way Ma liked them, like fife-and-drummers marching back-to-belly, not the way he and Pa had tossed them in while she was gone. James relished the clatter of the knives that dimmed Ma's ramblings.

"Thee must have some clever disguise for thy trip to Kentucky," Ma said. "Thee can't just travel willy-nilly."

"If he's to travel at all," Pa muttered. Now that brush angrily slapped across the boot.

The only other sound in the room was Ma mixing sarsaparilla. The grainy sugar scratched the bottom of the kettle. "Thee remembers the story Miss Elizabeth told about Ellen Craft? How she and her husband, William, escaped?"

Oh, no. She meant for him to travel all wrapped in a smelly poultice!

"Not me, Ma. It'll have to be Solomon larded with the poultice and wrapped to his ears like a mummy."

Ma only pretended to consider this, then quickly came up with her own plan. "Solomon can easily pass as thy caretaker, but it is *thee* who must be in disguise."

"Thee doesn't mean to dress me as a woman?" James said with a groan.

"The Bible frowns upon such a thing."

"But thee asked it of the Negroes all the time, fancying them up in Quaker women's gowns and hoods and all."

"For their safety, James."

"Ma, I can't sleep!" Rebecca shouted from upstairs. "It's too cold."

Ma went to the bottom of the stairs and answered in her normal voice. Ma never raised her voice, which made James want to yell like a banshee. "Take the comforter from James's bed, child. He'll be needing to get used to discomfiting conditions."

James heard Rebecca scurry across the floor to his room and back. He'd be wearing his overcoat to bed until he set out on his trip. Then an idea struck him: "Tell her, Pa. How can I go to Kentucky? I'll miss so much school." It was a feeble effort, he knew, for Ma had always put more stock in home-school than in those classes with Miss Malone a few months out of the year.

"The boy rightly raises a point, Mrs. Weaver."

Ma ignored him. "Oh, gracious, I nearly forgot thy presents, James. Thee must have presents on thy birthday, son." Ma dug deep into a carpetbag she'd tucked under the table. "Ah, here." She handed him a bundle of books tied with white wool.

The first was *Mitchell's Primary Geography*. James flipped it open to the page marked with a slip of Grandma Baylor's creamy stationery, and he read, "'Kentucky is noted for its caves. . . .'"

"Thee meant all along for me to go to Kentucky?" James asked.

"How could I? I didn't know we'd lost Miss Elizabeth. It's mere coincidence. Look what else is in the pile, son."

He turned over a book called *Walden*, by Henry David Thoreau. James fluttered the densely printed pages. As far as he could see, their only use would be as a fan in the summertime.

"Does thee dismiss Thoreau so easily? He's a man comfortable with silence."

And she knows I'm not, James thought.

"Mrs. Weaver, has thee come back a changeling?" Pa said. "Mr. Thoreau is not Moses, and *Walden* is surely not the Bible." The words seemed gentle enough, but James smelled anger in the room, thick as smoke.

"And thee'd profit from reading a chapter or two thyself, Mr. Weaver. However, this book I've

48

brought James has valuable things to say to us in modern times such as we live in. Thoreau implores us to live deliberately, not potluck."

Oh, mercy, here it comes. James half listened while he examined the other two books she'd handed him. Why, each had his name engraved in gold leaf on the puffy black leather binding. Inside were miles of beautiful blank pages.

Back at the stove, Ma stirred that sarsaparilla into a whirlwind. "It's time thee had proper sketchbooks if thee's to be a builder of great buildings."

His heart flew: page after page begging to be filled with his drawings!

"Oh, I'd almost forgotten." Ma laid the wooden spoon across the kettle and rummaged around in the carpetbag again. She pulled out a stack of pencils tied like a miniature cord of wood. "Does thee notice anything odd about these writing implements, James?"

Each had a pink stub at the end. He popped one in his mouth. It tasted of salt and stubborn rubber. "Could use a little flavor."

"It's not to eat, son. It's called an eraser, to scratch out what thee doesn't want on the page. Watch." Ma drew a squiggle on the first page of his sketchbook. *Spoiled it!* But then she rubbed that eraser over the mark, and it was gone. "Thy grandfather bought these in Boston for thee before—"

James swallowed a lump. "Well, of course before. He couldn't buy them after he was dead, Ma."

Ma studied his face a moment. "Thee takes death so lightly. I suppose that's youth."

How little she knew. Grandpa Baylor's death was like a gaping, jagged hole in his heart. He'd begun to sketch Grandpa Baylor's study in Boston until he'd realized that he no longer remembered the details of that room where he'd spent so much of his growing-up time. He remembered the books that lined the walls, and the maps rolled in the corner, standing like smokestacks, but little else. Well, no matter. He'd invent the room the way he saw it forming in his mind's eye.

Then their good friend, the free black man, Solomon Jefferson, arrived. One glance, and James knew Solomon had seen a ghost, or worse.

Solomon tipped his hat to Ma, not even pretending it was good to have her back after so many months. "Mr. Weaver, I got to have a word with you."

Pa put down the boot and looked nervously at Ma. She quickly got up and ran the wooden paddle through the sarsaparilla again, rattling that kettle all she could to give Pa and Solomon some privacy. She didn't miss a word, though, James could tell. As for him, he and Pa and Solomon had been a threesome all through the bitter winter, so he had a perfect right to listen in.

Solomon worked his fingers around the rim of his hat as he spoke low. "Dr. Olney, he just got a wire from his friend in Washington. Sent me over to tell you the news, Mr. Weaver." James saw him trying to miss Pa's eyes, which were searching for the news in Solomon's sad face.

"Say it outright, Solomon."

"Well, sir, the Supreme Court made their decision in the Dred Scott case."

Pa took up the fireplace poker, squeezing it tight enough to draw sap from it. "And what was the decision, sir?"

"Court said no Negro slave or descendant of one is a citizen of the United States."

Ma spun around, flicking sarsaparilla like gold dust. "Solomon Jefferson, thee's a free man and a citizen of a free territory."

"Yes, Miz Weaver, but that's not good enough, starting today. And now the Supreme Court says Congress has no right to stop slavery in the territories. I don't mean any disrespect, ma'am, but that includes Kansas Territory."

"Oh, piffle!" Ma said, brandishing that wooden paddle like a sword, not that Ma would *ever* take up a weapon. "Tell them, Mr. Weaver, thee's the legal expert here." But before Pa could say a word, Ma continued, "It's not been three years since Congress passed the Kansas-Nebraska Act granting us the right to vote whether we'll be Free State or slave. Why, there's not three God-fearing legitimate voters in all of Kansas Territory who'd vote for anything but freedom for *all* its citizens."

51

Pa led Ma to her rocker and directed Solomon to the bench nearby. He stood, stoking the dwindling fire. James knew they were in for a long siege on this one.

"Mrs. Weaver," Pa began, then eased up. "Millicent, dear, thee knows I've studied this case for the eleven years it's been working its way through the courts." He turned around to face Ma, and she nodded. "Today's decision renders the Kansas-Nebraska Act good as dead. Missouri Compromise, too. Am I right, Solomon?"

"Yes, sir."

"The news Solomon brings us is this." Pa stood tall and straight, drawing on his most lawyerly voice. "While the courts have held to the principle of *once free, always free,* today's decision now means *once a slave, always a slave.*"

James felt the tension seep into the kitchen like river sand streaming back into a hole.

"Well, then, Mr. Weaver," Ma said, biting the corner of her lip, "one thing's clear. James and Solomon must be on their way."

"Ma'am?" Solomon asked.

"After First Day, at dawn on Monday morning, on thy way to Kentucky."

"Pa!"

Pa put his arm around James and drew Solomon to him as well. "I believe it's the right thing to do, given this unsavory turn of events."

Ma's eyes flew from James to Pa, and her lip quivered just a bit. "Mr. Weaver," she said gently, "thee must explain the mission to Solomon. I've unpacking to attend to upstairs." Ma started for the stairs but just couldn't resist telling them all what to do. "I've thought on this, James, and prayed a good bit. Listen up, son. Thee shall go disguised as a feebleminded child returning to the plantation after doctoring in St. Louis. Solomon shall be thy caretaker."

"Truth be known, Miz Weaver, Lizbet had in mind for me to go after her folks in Kentucky, and I promised her. Miz Pru Biggers, her mother, she's been expecting Lizbet to come for her since winter. Sick as Lizbet was, with her head spinning like a whirligig, she propped herself up on a pillow and drew me this map." Solomon reached into his inside pocket and pulled out a sheaf of folded papers. "She told me just how to go; I wrote it all down like she said it." He spread the papers out for Ma and Pa to look at, and James craned his neck to get a peek as well. "Ever since we lost her, lost Lizbet, Miz Weaver, I've just been chewing on how to keep her promise."

Ma fidgeted, obviously touched by Solomon's words. Her voice hoarse, she said, "Well, then, it's settled." And it was done so easily, without so much as a nod of agreement from James. Had thirteen-year-olds no word in their own fate?

"Mr. Weaver?" Ma gave Pa a pleading look. "Has thee anything more to add?"

"I believe I said my piece earlier, Mrs. Weaver, both against and for thy scheme." James held his breath, his last hope. Pa rubbed his hands together until they screeched, while Solomon stood up with his hat over his heart. Pa's deep sigh rang like a bell in his throat, and he said, "Tomorrow I will draw up legal papers. Bogus papers, I might remind thee."

Ma nodded. "Thee is doing God's will. So, Solomon, thee must tell us about the Olneys. That baby would be nearly walking by now."

Halfheartedly Solomon delivered news of the Olneys and the other Quaker families as James swayed in Pa's rocker, erasing every mark in Grandpa Baylor's room that didn't belong on the page. In three days he'd be on the road, and who knew what danger lurked around the bends of the mighty Missouri River? He might never draw a room or a building again.

Chapter Thirteen
HOUND DOG PJ'S

The lovebirds, Mattie and Raymond Berk, were out to lunch, so I offered to make up their room.

Mom knelt in the recently invaded closet. Winter coats muffled her words: "Why, Dana Shannon, I'm stunned by your burst of responsibility."

"Yeah, that's me, the hyperresponsible one." The lockbox at the top of the stairs jangled as I rummaged around for the spare key.

The Berks' room looked like a battlefield. The down comforter with the patchwork duvet was in a heap on the floor, and the sheets were all loose and lumpy, as if a hamster had burrowed under them. Raymond's hound dog pj's lay on the floor beside some white socks that were accordioned. I kicked the ripe socks under the bed. Hershey's Kisses foil and Juicy Fruit gum wrappers were scattered like buckshot around the room.

On the floor next to the bed was a suitcase bursting with items: socks and underwear, Mattie's knitting, in a crinkly JCPenney bag, a red plaid blouse . . .

"Dana? You in there?" I jumped to my feet just as Mom pushed the door open with her elbows.

"These are the extra sheets that match the drapes in this room. Boy, what swine! There's something odd about these people, honey, you get that feeling?"

I shrugged. "They seem as normal as most adults."

"That's not saying much. Need some help?"

"I can handle it, Mom." I smiled and backed Mom toward the door, trying to act like I wasn't rushing her out so I could tear into the Berks' most private possessions. Once Mom was on her way downstairs, I locked the door as silently as I could and returned to the jumbled suitcase.

. . . a tacky white macramé belt, the navy slacks and football-shoulder magenta sweater, and an industrial-size bag of still more Hershey's Kisses, these in the gold wrappers, with almonds.

At the bottom of the pile was a thick manila envelope, fastened with one of those figure-eight string deals. *It isn't my business,* I reminded myself, but I opened the envelope, anyway. Inside were reproductions of old Kansas maps and color copies of pages from some coffee-table architecture book—all James Weaver buildings. There was Wolcott Castle, with its beautiful pink awnings and balconies and turrets. Also, there were pictures of a livestock exchange in Abilene and an African Methodist Episcopal church in Fort Scott.

Under them all was a bulky paper folded into eighths. The fold lines were well worn. I spread the paper out on the bed.

It was a blueprint of our house!

56

Chapter Fourteen
March 1857
A SURPRISE PASSENGER

A grapevine sweetened the crisp spring air. Pa held the reins tight on Buttermilk, who was anxious to be trotting James and Solomon off to their first stop. Ma, Rebecca, and the Olneys all stood on the porch waving them good-bye.

"Go with God, friends," Dr. Olney said. His red face puffed up over his ruffled collar. "Thee's in His hands. Yes, the Lord will keep a watchful eye on thee. Thee need never fear, for the Almighty shall guide thee." James saw Mrs. Olney elbow her husband to stop the rain of words pouring from him. "Well, madam," he said, wrinkling his brow. "A little benediction can't hurt. A blessing. A prayer. A fare-thee-well."

Pa said, "We'd best leave now if they're to make the coach to Kansas City."

Solomon was already in the wagon, and James climbed in beside the basket trunk that sat on the seat between them. He'd watched Ma and Mrs. Olney fill it with extra clothes for the fugitives, blankets, pillows, maps, and all sorts of food: fried prairie chicken, chicory coffee, pickled globe apples, sticks of maple sugar candy, hardtack, and a jar of fresh milk that, with all the shaking along the way, would churn itself into butter. Just the thought made the juices in James's stomach churn and clot.

Ma came to the wagon and spoke to Solomon. "Thee take care of the boy, hear? And trust him. He's not a pioneer, but he's a good and smart boy."

"Yes, ma'am, I know what James can do. Don't you worry, Miz Weaver."

"I suppose thee would know," Ma said, "what with the typhoid and all. Well." She tucked a blanket around James's knees. "Be strong, son." Her eyes were screwed to the size of nail heads, as if loosening them meant a tear might escape.

Rebecca clung to Ma's skirt, wailing for both of them. "What if I don't ever see James again? What if he's eaten by wolves? What if Indians catch him? There's Indians out there, not as nice as our own Delawares."

Ma clapped her hand over Rebecca's mouth. "Say farewell to thy brother and to Solomon," she commanded, then added under her breath, "or say nothing at all."

"Bye," Rebecca whined, waving the tips of her fingers.

"Remember all that I've told thee, son."

"Yes, Ma." She'd written dozens of details on his mind, and he knew he'd forget them all at the border of Missouri when things heated up.

Pa waved the reins, and just before Buttermilk took off, here came Will Bowers hobbling on his one leg and crutch. "Hey, wait up."

Ma asked, "Will, has thee come to say good-bye to thy friend?"

Will leaned on his crutch and doffed his hat. "No, ma'am. I'm going with him."

"Thee is not!" James protested. Why had he ever mentioned it to Will?

Will tossed his bag smack on James's feet, and he hopped into the wagon with amazing agility. He'd still not said a word to James, but to Ma he said, "Way I figure it, Mrs. Weaver, James will be a lamb in the jungle without I'm there to see him through."

James kicked the rucksack away and fumed; a smile played on Solomon's lips, until Will finished his thoughts: "And I reckon Solomon can use a hand that's had some fighting experience. From what I've seen of James and Solomon, neither one's likely to hold up against a real enemy."

The wagon was a two-seater, plus one for Pa, plus the basket trunk, so Will ripped the blanket away and dropped to the floor between James's and Solomon's feet. He pulled his half-leg into place since it seemed not to get the message from his brain on its own.

Pa held the reins tight again and leaned back.

"Will, thee's sure thee wants to do this?"

"Sure as locusts, sir."

Ma had a different concern. "Will Bowers, this is not a merry adventure. This is a sacred mission. Thee must not compromise the safety of Miss Elizabeth Charles's Negroes who have dreamed all winter of making free."

"Ma'am, all due respect, I've been with John Brown over in Pottawatomie, and there's no man on God's earth with his eye more fixed on ending slavery."

James saw Ma's lips twist. She didn't approve of using the Lord's name in vain, and she *surely* didn't approve of John Brown. She'd grant that he was a rebel for the right cause, just as she was, but he used the wrong means. He hadn't a qualm about wielding guns and knives and even a broadax. Ma pulled in air and gave Will one of her looks that bored to the heart of you, sure as an awl. "Guard thy inclinations, son." She stepped away from the wagon and smiled thinly. "Caleb, be sure thee's back in time for dinner. It shall be lonesome around our table tonight."

Pa snapped the reins and gave Buttermilk the signal. "Watch our dust, Mrs. Weaver."

"Never mind. I'll watch for thy return, that's what. Oh, and Mr. Weaver, don't drive that horse as if thee were in a chariot race."

✳ ✳ ✳

Pa delivered them to the stagecoach just on time. Solomon fixed himself on the bench across from James and Will. The papers that proved he was a free man were in a leather pouch clutched to his chest.

Pa handed James an identical pouch. "In here are legal papers proving that Solomon is a slave owned by me, and also passes entitling a slave of his description to travel."

"Pa!"

"Hush, son. Thee doesn't know what lies ahead on thy journey, and Solomon is prepared for this. One day thee might have to prove that he's free, and another day thee might need to be a young master and Solomon thy loyal servant."

"We'll handle it, Mr. Weaver," Will said.

Pa nodded, but looked right past Will. "Does thee understand, son¿ James¿"

"Yes, sir," James said with a sigh.

Pa pressed fifty dollars into his hand and gave Solomon fifty dollars as well, but Solomon protested. "Dr. Olney staked me, sir."

"Would thee decline money borrowed from Mrs. Weaver's cookie jar¿ She'd not let me back in the house, friend."

Solomon smiled and tucked the money in his black coat pocket.

There was a great rustle and cascading of skirts as a lady tried to hoist herself up into the coach. The driver actually had to shove her from behind.

"Fresh man!" she squealed. Her skirt, with hoop and bustle, just about filled what was left of the space. "Oh, I see the cabin's occupied." Then she spied Solomon. "Well! My daddy didn't rear me to ride with the likes of *him*."

"Madam," Pa began, but Solomon slung his pouch over his shoulder and said, "I'm just settling the boy in, ma'am. Don't mind me. I'll be riding up with the driver."

James had no wish to travel with this rude woman, but Solomon had climbed onto the seat next to the driver, who was calling for departure, and now Pa was firing a volley of last-minute instructions:

"Be careful. Don't talk to anybody unless thee knows they're trustworthy. Heed Solomon's advice, but use thy own head. Send thy mother letters as often as possible. She'll be worrying, son. Take care, Will. Thee might write thy mother, as well."

Pa shook their hands and tipped his hat to the lady. He dropped one foot behind him onto the step of the coach and said, "James, mind thee isn't drawing pictures when thee needs to be alert." Gravely, he added, "Son, thee will need to be very alert." He stepped down and slammed the door shut.

James lurched forward as the coach took off. The bench was plenty wide enough for him and Will both, but he didn't dare look at Will because they'd both burst out laughing at the woman across from them with her grin that cracked her thick makeup. James smiled at her. Her eyes flared, and she kept that grin fixed on James until he thought he'd spit. *Doesn't she ever have to blink?* He glanced at Will, who was already dozing, and at the red velvet walls and the black leather seats, but there wasn't much to study in this small coach since *she* took up most of it.

"What's happened to your friend's leg?" she whispered.

"Lost it," James said simply. No point in giving her the grisly details.

"Rather careless of him, wasn't it? You seem like a nice enough boy. Going back to school in Philadelphia? One can't possibly learn letters and numbers out here in the wilds."

"No, ma'am. I'm headed for St. Louis to see a doctor. Him, too."

She looked at James sharply, a handkerchief pressed to her painted lips. "Surely you're not sick. You look positively hale and ready to tame a stallion."

James took off his hat and tapped his temple. "It's in here, ma'am." He made his eyes wide and wild and pulled his hair into spikes like short wheat stalks. "I'm stark-raving mad!"

"Oooh," she gasped. "Wouldn't you just know it. I'm to ride all day to Kansas City, thirty-five countless miles, over these primitive pioneer ruts,

63

with a lunatic, a cripple, and a darky. I ought never to have left Philadelphia. God preserve."

James bared his teeth, which were none too straight and were a little scary even on a good day. He watched her shrink into a corner of her bench, with her hoop standing straight up.

Sure now that she wouldn't talk him to death, he took out his sketchbook and one of those amazing eraser pencils and began to draw the countryside streaming past him. Will snored.

Chapter Fifteen
SAMUEL STRAIGHTFEATHER

Odd little symbols like suture tracks dotted the blueprint of our house. I really wanted to slip that blueprint right out of the room. But they'd find out soon enough and have a fit, and I'd be in capital Trouble with my parents, so I put all the papers back and refastened the envelope. Sliding it under the clothes, I felt something that was fat and squishy—a small book packed in thick Bubble Wrap. Who could resist? I popped a couple of those bubbles while I argued with myself, but I lost the argument and ended up unwrapping an old book called *Delaware: Land and People*. Bits of sparkly brown dye from the binding came off in my hand as I opened the book. Its yellowed pages had hairline tears. The book had to be at least a hundred years old, although there was no copyright date on the title page.

Now, why would the Berks be carrying an old book about Delaware? Did they plan to pawn it or sell it to an antique dealer? I carefully turned page after page, corners crumbling to powder in my fingers. If I wasn't careful, the book would end up filling a mayonnaise jar. It fell open in the middle for a glossy picture of the author, Samuel Straightfeather, in full Indian dress. He was surrounded by a bevy of white men wearing old-fashioned business suits and bowlers. The caption read, STRAIGHTFEATHER PLEADS FOR HIS PEOPLE'S LAND AMONG PRESIDENT BUCHANAN'S AGENTS. LAWRENCE, KANSAS, MARCH 1857.

Not Delaware, the state; Delaware, the *Indians!* But what were they to the Berks—kin? I tried to reconstruct the Berks' faces in my mind, scanning for signs of a square jaw or high-colored skin or sleek black hair. No, they seemed like they could be my relatives, not Samuel Straightfeather's.

But obviously this book was important to them. What did it have to do with their prowling around our house? Were they actually on Indian business and not James Weaver business? What kind?

There was a key in the lock, and the doorknob was turning. I stuffed the book back into the suitcase, but there wasn't time to slip it into the Bubble Wrap. Just as the door swung open, I yanked the sheets off the bed like one of those tricks where you whip off the tablecloth and leave all the dishes and glasses in place.

"What are you doing in here?" Mr. Berk asked. His harsh voice rocked me back on my heels.

"Just tidying up," I sweetly replied, but my heart was pounding.

Mr. Berk put on his exaggerated limp for my

benefit. "Listen, just leave the fresh sheets and towels. Me and the missus will take care of it ourselves."

"But it's part of the bed-and-breakfast service; it's our pleasure—"

"Yeah, well, my pleasure is to take a long, hot shower to clear out my sinuses and go back to bed. I'm coming down with it." He stepped forward and coughed directly in my face. "Sorry."

I glanced at the suitcase. The book was showing. I dropped to the floor. My left hand stuffed the book back under the magenta sweater, and my right closed over something stiff and clammy under the bed. Holding my breath, I said, "Oh, look, your socks, Mr. Berk."

Close call! I didn't breathe again until I could take a refreshing whiff of the potpourri on the hall table.

As soon as I could get away, I'd go to the library and read up on the Delaware Indians. Kiowa I knew about, and Pawnee and Shawnee and Apache, but I couldn't remember one single thing about the Delaware.

But I should know about them, because James did, and he and I had some weird, coppery-wire link that stretched from his century to mine.

What did the Delaware Indians have to do with James Weaver?

Chapter Sixteen
March 1857
DELAWARE WOMAN

The coach bounced along the rutted road for about half an hour, until James thought his brains were sloshing around inside his head. Across from Will and him, Miss Farrell, the lady, was green, even with all that makeup. Her jowls flapped in the jarring rhythm of the coach.

All day like this, James thought, and then disaster—or was it luck?—befell them. The four-horse team refused the urging of the driver to bypass a mighty pothole, and they tore straight ahead into it. James felt the soft earth suck them in until the two right wheels were up to the hub in mud and the horses on that side were up to their flanks. James was practically lying on his right side, Will smashed against him, while Miss Farrell jammed one hefty boot across the bench to brace herself.

But two wheels and two horses weren't stuck, and those horses were chomping to get going. All four were whinnying at one another. The mud-deep horses won the battle. They simply lay down on a hard patch of ground and pulled the wagon over until horses and passengers were caddywampus and the baggage and Will's crutch were thrown into the bushes that were just bursting with new spring greenery.

Miss Farrell landed on top of James and Will, and her hoops just about swallowed them up. "I never!" she cried as they tried to push her off, but she probably weighed more than the two of them combined.

Now Solomon and the driver were pulling on the horses to stand the wagon back up, but all the animals were spooked and the coach was a hopeless wreck. A wheel had broken off and rolled into a ravine, and the door hung by one hinge like a flap of skin.

"I quit!" yelled the driver. "Two months driving this thang until my kidneys is loose in my belly, and they don't pay me but a slave's wages, which ain't enough to keep my dogs any meat on their bones, let alone my wife and children. Out, all of you."

James and Will and Miss Farrell tumbled out onto the solid earth. James helped Will up and propped him against a tree. The driver collected their baggage, kicked a wheel coated with mud, handed Will his crutch, and pointed through the trees. "Yer in luck. Through there's the river, and they's a Frenchman's got a Delaware wife runs a flatboat across the river." He handed them back the three and a half dollars they'd each paid and grinned mischievously. "Have an elegant trip, folks!"

James and Solomon carried their trunk between them, and Solomon also dragged the lady's trunk while she showed fat limbs by lifting her skirts out of the mud and thistle.

Will outdistanced them quickly and reported back. "Look yonder, the flatboat."

The flatboat was tied to a cottonwood tree on the north bank of the Kansas River, and to another tree on the south bank. A system of pulleys and winches got that contraption across, helped along by the force of the river current.

The flatboat owner gladly took their money and loaded the four of them on the boat.

"He expects me to sit right out here under God and the sun?" Miss Farrell asked. She pulled the rim of her hat over her face, as though her hide would molt if it got a little sun. But at least she wasn't upset anymore to be riding with Solomon, for she gladly clung to his arm as the pulleys cranked and the boat started moving.

Suddenly a man streaked through the redbuds and cottonwoods and grabbed the rope that anchored the boat. He waved a bowie knife; sunlight gleamed off of it in blinding flickers. "The Frenchman, he ain't got no charter to ferry people crost this river. I do, two miles down."

His throat just inches from the knife, the Frenchman yelled in his own language. He was probably cussing, but his English was better than the ferryman's. "My wife's people are the Delaware, and they own the land this side of the river, friend."

"Ya ain't own the south bank," the ferryman said, using that knife as a pointer.

"No, sir," the Frenchman said, calm as could be. "Not anymore. But if you have a right to Delaware Trust Land on the north bank of the river, then the Delaware have a right to white man's land on the south. Fair play?"

"Listen, mister, I got the charter from the U.S. government, and you ain't even a citizen *or* a red man. You four on that boat, I'm warning you, load off or I'm cutting the rope that ties this piece of cork you're floating on, and y'all will drift downstream, want to or not." He raised the knife to the rope, and Miss Farrell screamed.

"Throw down that knife!" An Indian woman came into the clearing, aiming a shotgun right at the ferryman.

"Whoa," he yelled, backing into the trees.

"Nice to see you, darlin'," the Frenchman said as his wife climbed aboard and tucked her shotgun under a blanket. The Frenchman yanked on the rope and sent them all floating across the Kansas River to the grinding sound of the pulleys. Not twenty minutes later, he and his wife were smooching on the north bank.

"Look at those two," Will grumbled. "Kinda makes you sick at your stomach."

Hundreds of people waited with James and Will to board steamboats and to see travelers off on their journey along the Missouri River, which was nicknamed "the Big Muddy." Solomon stood away from the crowd, even apart from the other Negro passengers, and a quick glance told James he was plumb scared to venture out of Kansas Territory. James had never known Solomon to be scared, even that time he'd been dragged off by a slave catcher, and it pained James sorely now. Why, Solomon was just about the best friend he had.

Miss Farrell entertained the crowd with a tail about her French poodle, demonstrating how Pierre pranced on his spindly legs; her hoops and skirts swayed like wheat in a storm. James watched Solomon relax a bit with Miss Farrell's silly prattling.

The steamboat would be heading for St. Louis, where the Missouri joined the Mississippi and flowed from there to exotic southern ports James had only heard of, like Natchez and New Orleans.

James hooked his coat on his thumb over his shoulder, as the day had grown warm and humid for March. He watched passengers from the *Western Star* languidly disembark on the Missouri shore. People greeted them with hugs and handshakes, and for a flash James felt a pang of homesickness, even for the bratty Rebecca.

Then Will said, "Psst, James, over here." Will had caught sight of a very different sort of greeting as immigrants from the east claimed their wagons and oxen. A band of Missouri Border Ruffians held the men at bay with pistols while their confederates smashed locks on the trunks and crates. They slashed baskets and bags. Flour poured like water. Beans and rice clattered onto the dusty ground. Sewing notions and medicine bottles and gimcracks of every kind tumbled out and rolled all over while the owners gasped at the wreckage of their life's accumulation.

"No way are you Yankees bringing this stuff into Kansas," one frenzied man yelled, and another said, "Hobie, look. I found me a cache of Beecher's Bibles."

James recognized the code name for Sharps rifles, repeating guns meant for the defenders of Lawrence.

A third man held a billowy red dress up to his torso and did a little dance. "Molly Ruth's gonna look right pretty in this, reckon?"

One of the men guarding the owners yelled, "Quit your sporting, men, we've got work to do." They began herding the passengers into a tight circle like sheep.

"Go get your women and children if you want to wake up anything but dead tomorrow. Y'all are taking another trip, back east."

One brave soul shouted, "We've come across the country, and we mean to settle in the Free State of Kansas."

"Oh, yeah?" Dry earth rushed up and blinded the men when one of the ruffians fired a couple of shots into the ground. More shots ricocheted off the ground, and the Eastern men ran for cover.

Will tamped the ground around those gunshots. "Who put you men up to this?"

Oh, no! Why did he have to open his mouth?

"What did you say, boy?"

"I asked, who are you working for?"

A big man with a buffalo mane of white hair stepped forward and hung his huge frame over Will. James's heart jumped as he inched closer, but for what? He didn't know the first thing to do as the pot began to boil.

"You soft on slavery, boy?"

Will stood his ground, that sack of leg swinging just as if a light breeze rocked a porch chair. "Yes, sir, I am."

"Well, listen here, boy. If you've got a mind to steal you a few Nigras from their rightful owners and haul them over the border into Kansas, well, boy, you can count on this: Me and a thousand like me will be here waiting for you."

The buffalo man seemed to notice James for the first time. "You, sissy-boy, you a fancy slave-stealer, too?"

"No, sir," James said. Lying didn't come easily to him, but he remembered Ma saying, "One man cannot own another," and so what they'd be doing with the runaways couldn't be stealing. "I'd never steal property. Sir." Again, Ma's voice: "James, people are not chattel. They are human beings, with souls that belong to God."

The mean man glared at Will. "This boy your friend?"

Will pivoted on his heel. "Who, him? I never saw him in my life."

James swallowed a lump in his throat the size of a crab apple.

The man waved his gun. "Git, both of you, go on."

Will raced his crutch to the end of the loading dock, and James made himself walk slowly, as if he had nothing to hide. But he did have something to hide: a huge ball of fear knotting in his stomach like the eye of a storm.

Will found him when they were out of sight of the brigands. "Well, you didn't get all lily-livered back there with that wild man."

"Felt lily-livered, though."

"Who cares what you feel, James? It's what you show that counts."

"I'm never going to have thy kind of courage."

Will pulled an apple out of his rucksack. In three massive bites he was down to the core. "Come on.

We're about ready to board our gentlemen's ship. Might as well have a good time while we can, 'cause one thing's for sure: We've got some rough days ahead." Will swallowed the sinewy core, seeds and stem and all. "Sure will take a long time. Months, maybe."

Chapter Seventeen
NO HULA HOOPS

"Hello, Dana¿" Mike had put on his telephone voice, which was a full octave lower than his school voice. "Listen, this isn't about a date or anything."

My heart somersaulted. "Who said anything about a date¿"

"It's just a Bat Mitzvah thing."

"You're not Jewish, Mike."

"My cousin Sarah is. She's having a huge party at the Doubletree in Overland Park."

"So, what's the not-a-date part¿" I was filing a rough spot on my thumbnail, and the raspy sound made me feel squeamish. Or was it the conversation¿

"Sarah's inviting about fifty kids, mostly little seventh graders, and I won't know anybody, and I'll sit there like a hermit, so I thought you could come and make me look normal."

"No way. Ask Sally."

"I already did. She swore at me."

"And now you're asking me¿ I'm insulted. What about Ahn¿" I had to be careful I didn't talk him out of this.

"Her brothers would never let her go. Besides,

77

how do I explain a Buddhist to my Jewish and Christian relatives?"

"So, let me get this straight. I'm the least offensive of your female friends?" I tapped the phone furiously with my nail file, trying to remember why I thought Mike was cute. After an embarrassing silence, I asked, "Mike? You alive over there?"

"It was just a wild thought. You don't have to go. I don't even have to go. I'll just say I have rabies or something."

"Okay, okay, what's involved?"

"Dancing."

"I'm not dancing with you!"

"Nobody says we have to dance. But I've got to warn you, Sarah will have a sappy DJ who engineers games like Hula Hoop and limbo contests."

"Absolutely no Hula Hoops, you understand?"

"I'd rather eat sawdust. What about the limbo?"

"Possibly. Will there be food?"

"Mountains of it, and Pepsi flowing like the Mississippi."

"When is it?" I asked, as though I were inquiring about a public hanging.

"A week from Saturday night."

"I'll ask my parents." Of *course* they'd say yes. The place would be loaded with parents. Mine wouldn't be able to resist sending me off to a safe, religious, family celebration like this, since they are already worried that I am a social misfit, the kind who stays home on weekends to dissect crickets or cook marzipan.

"What do I have to wear?" I'd grown three inches since Christmas and don't have knees to model in *Vogue* with.

"You've got some kind of dress, don't you?"

"I'll go to the Salvation Army store," I said dryly.

"That'll work. Thanks. You saved me from looking like a moron."

His words sounded humble, but I could just see the grin of triumph spread across his face. I had a hungry urge to rub it off. "So, Mike, now you owe me big." Time to come in for the kill!

"Anything. Whatever it is, I'm going to hate it."

"Definitely. It involves getting your brother to drive you and Jeep and me to Kansas City and asking a lot of probing questions about Ernie's Bait Shop and the Berks, and maybe even breaking into their house."

"Wait a minute. I could wind up in jail. This is way more than I owe you."

I was glad he couldn't see my gloating sneer. "Right. So ask Sally to go to the stupid party, or ask Celina, that cheerleader who makes your ears turn red."

"You're cruel!" Mike slammed the phone down, then called right back. "When do you want to go?"

"Tomorrow afternoon."

"So soon? I don't have time to get mentally prepared."

"Tomorrow," I said firmly. "At two o'clock."

Chapter Eighteen
March 1857
THE CUTEST THANG!

The *Francie Mulryan* showed off like a dazzling queen along the bank of the Missouri. Her smoke-stacks poked into the clear blue, and her side-wheels churned water as her decks filled with passengers in all kinds of spring finery.

The baggage had already been loaded onto the steamboat. James, Will, and Solomon waited in line to board. Solomon held their tickets out for the agent, while Miss Farrell fumbled around in her enormous carpetbag for her ticket. She thrust it into Solomon's hand. "I just can't mind details," she said.

"Ma'am, I don't think—," Solomon protested.

"Of course you don't," Miss Farrell said. "You've not had the experience."

James had put up with quite enough. "Miss Farrell, ma'am, thee must hear a thing or two about Solomon Jefferson here. He's a free man, born free in Boston, Massachusetts, and he's lived free all his life."

Solomon tapped James on his shoulder, but James shrugged him off.

"He's been to school. I reckon he can read about as well as thee."

"If you can read at all," Will muttered.

Miss Farrell bit her finger, and tears welled up in her eyes, until James felt a twinge of remorse, but not enough to say *I'm sorry*. He nudged Solomon, and they stepped away from the woman.

She wasn't about to let them escape, though; she sidled right up between James and Will. "You must think me a heartless sow."

"You ain't heartless," Will said, and James quickly drowned his words: "We forgive thee."

While Miss Farrell dabbed at her eyes, Solomon whispered, "James, sir, you'd best stop saying *thee* and *thy*. Nobody's going to believe you're a Southern gentleman if you talk like that William Shakespeare man."

James nodded and practiced *you* and *your* in his head. It sounded so common, so coarse. When they got to the front of the line, the steamboat agent asked, "This black man got a pass to travel?"

"No need, sir," Solomon answered.

"Was I talking to you?" The burly agent addressed his comments to Miss Farrell. "Is he your slave, missus?"

"Oh, land's sake, no. I'm a Philadelphia woman. We don't keep slaves in the North, goodness no."

"Whose slave is he, then? Soon as the boat loads, I'd be glad to see him home to Louisiana, or is it Mississippi? I could make me a pretty penny."

Solomon looked down at the ground and softly said, "I live in Lawrence, Kansas, sir, on free soil. I'm a free man." He lifted the flap on his leather pouch for proof, but the man must have thought Solomon was reaching for a weapon, because he jumped on Solomon's back and wrestled him to the ground. The passengers behind stepped back and formed a wide circle.

James made a snap decision and said in his most commanding voice, "Sir, let my man up."

Will poked the agent away with his crutch, and Solomon scrambled to his feet. He opened his pouch while James said, "Might I see thy badge, *your* badge, sir? Ah, Mr. Tully, allow me to introduce myself. I'm James Baylor Weaver, of Owensboro, Kentucky, and this is my brother, Will. Our father is Caleb Weaver, owner of a tobacco plantation."

Miss Farrell said, "Why, I thought—"

James kicked her ankle. "Solomon's our bondsman, third generation in our family. If it would make you rest easier, I can produce legal papers to that effect." James pulled a document out of his pouch and offered it to Tully.

At that very moment, Solomon also thrust his free papers into Tully's hand. Tully shoved his glasses down to the tip of his nose to study Solomon's papers.

"This sure enough says he's free." Then he looked at James's papers. "This sure enough says he's not." He looked from James to Solomon. "Now, I ask you, what's an honest, God-fearing man to believe?"

"Oh, I can explain," said Miss Farrell. "The boy's plain mad." She cupped her hand around her mouth and whispered good and loud, "He's not got his bait just right on the hook, if you understand my meaning. In fact, the child's on his way to see a doctor in St. Louis, and so's the lame one. It would be a tragedy if you didn't let them and their trusty servant board, sir, as the doctor could make a difference in whether this boy ends up in an asylum or the other one gets a peg leg."

"Who are you?" the agent asked.

"Alma Farrell, the boys' governess. I know I look like too fine a lady to be part of a domestic staff, but looks can be deceiving." She fluttered her eyelashes, and the agent blushed.

Tully was thoroughly bamboozled now. Free or slave? Madman or free man? Owensboro, Philadelphia, or Lawrence? Shaking his head, he handed Miss Farrell both sets of papers, took all four tickets, and let them board the *Francie Mulryan*.

Once safely onboard, Miss Farrell pulled a Chinese fan from her carpetbag and said, "Well, that's about the most fun I've had since the day my daddy had a pickle barrel topple over on him at

Hannibal's Saloon! I do admire a good lie now and then."

"Peg leg?" Will said. "I ain't a pirate, Miss Farrell, ma'am."

The first two days on the river passed pleasantly. James and Will shared a cabin that was fancier than any place James had ever slept. Meals in the dining room were elegant affairs, with forks and knives as heavy as hammers, and tablecloths starched so stiff, they crackled when your knee brushed against them.

Solomon was a deck passenger, along with other Negroes, wagons, and teams of horses and oxen. And because there were some three hundred passengers aboard, no one had seen Miss Farrell for two blessed days.

The spring rain had been sparse so far, and patches of the winter's ice hadn't melted yet, so the shallow water presented headaches for the captain of the *Francie Mulryan*. On the third day out, the boat edged up to the shore, and the captain announced, "All able-bodied boys over twelve and men under fifty will be getting out here."

"What?" Will demanded. "We're not *there* yet, are we?"

"We'll never make it over the sandbars in this shallow water," the captain said, "unless we lighten the load."

"How long are we going to have to walk?" an angry gentleman asked.

"Oh, no more than five, six miles," the captain assured him.

Will scrambled to be among the men disembarking, but James firmly said no. "There will be plenty of time for walking on the way back from Kentucky. Save thy shoe leather."

Will put up a weak battle. "You leaving me here with the women and children?" But he reluctantly agreed. He said the humidity from the river made his empty leg ache something fierce.

Two hours up the river, the men could all board again, and James found Will with a showgirl perched on his good knee and her arms around his skinny neck. "You're just the cutest thang!" the girl said.

"Somebody had to look after them," he told James.

Later, Will found a place at the poker table and coaxed James to sit down. "There's no sin in just watching." But James wasn't so sure. Ma did not approve of gambling, and, anyway, the game was puzzling. Those men drank spirits and said things like *hit me,* but nobody did, and *one-eyed jacks are wild,* but nobody seemed the least bit wild. They didn't say anything at all normal that James could understand, like *Mighty tough mutton this noon, eh?*

Will had a nice colorful stack of chips in front of

him, more than anybody else at the table except for one man who had flared cuffs and a lacy bib down his shirt and diamond studs for buttons. His face never moved except for a throb at his temple like a silent drumbeat. Only his eyes spoke, and the dealer always seemed to know what he was saying, though James had no idea what language he was speaking.

Behind them, a band played "My Old Kentucky Home" and "I Dream of Jeannie with the Light Brown Hair." Children danced to "Pop Goes the Weasel." James imagined Rebecca's head bobbing in the crowd, her cheeks red, her dress all askew, as the band slid into "Listen to the Mockingbird."

Bored with the poker game, James glanced out the window of the saloon and saw several Negroes dancing on the deck to the music, which must have come through only faintly to them.

Among the dancers, Solomon stood as still as a fence post. *He misses his sweetheart,* James thought. And as much as Miz Lizbet used to rile James with her stubborn *amen*s and her disgusting cures for freckles—buttermilk and manure, indeed!—James had to admit he missed her just a little bit, too. Now he wondered what her people in Kentucky had in mind for him.

Chapter Nineteen
RONALD McDONALD CURLS

That night I held vigil again, waiting for Raymond and Mattie to make their big move.

Their radio was tuned to a thirties big-band station. Ordinarily this corny music would have been jumbled with Jay Leno streaming out from under my parents' door, but Mom and Dad were at the Cervettis' with other history faculty couples for a wild evening of Pictionary and Trivial Pursuit.

This is pitiful, I thought. *I'm spending Saturday night alone with a jelly jar pressed to the wall. Get a life.* Then I reminded myself that at least I'd be doing the limbo next Saturday night on my nondate with my nonboyfriend, so I jumped off the bed and opened the folding shutters of my closet to see what might qualify as an actual party dress. Scraping hangers across the rack, I eliminated one ugly, wrong-color, too-short, too-tight specimen after another. But I made a useful discovery: I could hear Mattie and Raymond much more clearly from in the closet.

"Raymond, I told you to keep the book in the Bubble Wrap. The dye flakes are all over my clothes."

"Think, Mattie. When have you ever seen me open that book?"

"Then who was in our stuff?"

"The teenage bombshell with the Ronald McDonald curls."

I cringed. Was there time to get a haircut before next Saturday? I missed a few words, then caught Raymond: "I had a feeling the brat wasn't just doing the maid service number when I came back this morning. Mark my words, Mattie, if I catch that redhead messing with my stuff again, I'll break every bone in her scrawny body."

I heard a sluicing sound—Raymond imitating my bones snapping, one by one. My stomach flip-flopped, and I pulled myself in tighter, into a safe package. My ear was still pressed to the wall.

"You think she saw everything?" I heard a lot of rustling of papers and imagined Mattie inspecting the contents of the manila envelope. "I can't tell."

"It's not like you could pick up DNA tracings, Mattie."

"You're getting hostile, Raymond."

"We've gotta find it tonight. It's in the wall of one of the closets, that's what that moron Ernie's best guess is. Send a boy to do a man's job."

"Thank you, Arnold Schwarzenegger."

Raymond apparently decided to ignore her comment. "We know for a fact it's not the hall closet. I hit every inch of it before—"

"Before the mousetrap tragedy struck."

I couldn't make out his rumbling response, but it was clear this romance wasn't *Romeo and Juliet*.

I closed my closet and lay on the floor watching the shadows under the door. Were they dangerous? Could a man who got his toe caught in a mousetrap actually come after me? Then I heard again the sickening sound Raymond had made—my bones cracking like eggs, like pencils. I knew I'd hear that sound over and over in my sleep, in my dreams. Yes, they were dangerous.

I propped my eyes open with my fingers to keep from falling asleep and dreaming. I reminded myself that *to be awake is to be alive,* if I wanted to live *deliberately,* but somehow I drifted off, anyway, and woke with the pattern of the carpet pocking my cheek and a dust ball in my mouth. I could have missed something important!

I inched my door open. No one was in the hall. I tiptoed over to the bathroom, where I thought I saw a pinpoint of darting light, although it could have been the low-wattage night-light in a socket close to the floor.

Slowly, I pushed the bathroom door open. Something blocked it. I pushed harder. The door was slammed in my face!

Chapter Twenty
March 1857
THE FATHER OF WATERS

Miss Farrell tracked James down to say good-bye at St. Louis, where she was to board a train for Philadelphia. "Why, you're not even packed up. Aren't you and the others getting off here, too?"

"No, ma'am," James said. "We're heading down the Mississippi until it hits the Ohio."

"What about the doctor who's waiting for you in St. Louis?"

He shook his head.

"Then you're going on to Owensboro to see your mama and daddy?"

Again, he shook his head.

"Why, James Weaver, you rascal, you. That one-legged boy and the Negro and you, you're all going to Kentucky to help some slaves escape, aren't you? You're not raving mad at all."

"I'm sorry I lied to thee. To *you,* I mean."

"Ah-ah." She put her finger over his lips. "I tell you, it's been a lark. Say, we should exchange tokens." She buried her head in her carpetbag and pulled out a vial of something wet. "Smelling salts," she explained. "In case one of your runaways should faint. Oh, land's sake, you brave baby, you." She pouted. "I bet you don't have anything to give poor Alma Farrell."

"I do, ma'am." He slid a page of his sketchbook out and handed her the drawing he'd done of her. All the wrinkles were gone, along with about fifty pounds of flab.

She squinted to study the picture. "Why, I'm even lovelier than I imagined!" She planted a juicy kiss on James's cheek. He couldn't wait until her back was turned so he could wipe the greasy red mess away before somebody saw it.

He watched her promenade down the gangplank. Her skirt swayed like a bridge; and the gangplank buckled, then sprang back into place once she was on land.

Every day the captain of the *Francie Mulryan* called the passengers together for a little geography lesson.

"Here we go again," Will muttered, but James noticed that he absorbed each fact as though it were salve on a wound.

"Now that you're sailing the mighty Mississippi," the captain announced, "every lady and gentleman aboard my ship ought to know what the Algonquin called this miraculous river. Any guesses?"

Will shouted out, "'The Father of Waters.'"

"How did you know that, son?" asked the captain, clearly irritated.

"Says so right on my map."

"Ahem. Yes. Well. Here soon we'll be in Cairo, Illinois, where the Father of Waters meets the Ohio. Some of you good folks will be leaving us and sailing farther down into the south, but the proud *Francie Mulryan* will be steering north along the Kentucky border before we dip south again a short stitch into Paducah. Then, folks, you're on your own. Me, I get three days' vacation before I start this river circle all over again. There's a little woman waiting for me in Paducah," he said with a wink. "Well, the truth is, she's not so little, but she's my wife of thirty-two years, and I'm kind of used to her." People laughed politely. "Dis*missed,*" he said, as though he were the captain of a battleship instead of this floating palace, and they, his loyal crew, gladly dispersed.

Heading up to the deck for a game of mumblety-peg, Will said, "We should get off in Cairo. It's too risky going even the short distance to Paducah. Slave catchers are just itching to get their hands on the likes of Solomon."

James shook his head. "Paducah," he insisted. "We've got it all worked out to keep Solomon safe beside us. We'll do it after supper, when people wander out here on the deck. Does thee remember what to do?"

Will nodded, but he sure didn't look optimistic.

92

The utter perfection of the night helped. The moon was full and as yellow as butter. Stars hung from the sky like flickering Christmas candles. Lots of passengers had a yen to stroll in the moonlight, for there wasn't a whisper of wind; the plan wouldn't work on a windy night, of course. When a good crowd had assembled, James began to twirl in an ever-widening circle.

"What's the boy doing?" someone asked.

"Do you suppose he's got the Holy Spirit in him?" asked another.

"More likely the devil."

James pretended not to hear them. He stumbled over to the railing and climbed to its ledge, which was just wide enough for his shoe. "Look, I can fly!"

"Get down, you fool," Will yelled.

"Thee's just jealous because thee can't fly." He pointed to an old dowager. "Lady, can thee fly?"

"My word!" she shouted.

"Mister, can thee fly? I mean, can *you* fly? I think not, none of you have wings. But I have." James flapped his arms as the boat rocked gently.

"Somebody send for the captain!"

Two strong men carefully approached James, and not a moment too soon, because he opened his eyes and saw the black river swirling below, and his courage was slipping away. In slow synchronization, the men reached out and wrapped their arms around James's legs until he folded over the back of one of them, flapping his wings like a crazed vulture. "I can fly! I can fly!"

The captain appeared ondeck, still buttoning his shirt. "What's the ruckus?"

Will said, "Captain, sir, I'm afraid my brother has slipped out of his head again. Does it every four, five days. It's worse on full-moon nights like this. But, don't worry, we're taking him home to our pa."

"Look, Captain, I can fly! I can fly!" James shouted.

"For God's sake, calm the lad down," the captain commanded.

"Can't," said Will. "The only person on this boat who can talk to James when he gets this way is Solomon Jefferson."

"Well, where is the man?" asked the captain. "Bring him out here before this boy does mortal damage to himself and my boat."

"Sir, Solomon Jefferson is a black man. You don't cotton to having black folks mingling with white folks on the *Francie Mulryan*."

"This is an emergency. Somebody locate that Negro."

And that's how it happened that Solomon was allowed to stay in their cabin and by their side every remaining minute of the journey, until two days later when they docked at Paducah, Kentucky, and the *real* madness began.

Chapter Twenty-One
SILENT SCREAM

Shaking outside the bathroom door, I gasped when the door crept open a few inches and an arm reached out. Raymond Berk crooked his arm around my neck and slapped his hand across my mouth. He kicked the bathroom door open and yanked me inside. I stumbled across a heap of rubble on the floor. The claw-foot bathtub broke my fall with a punishing thrust to my stomach.

Raymond twisted my arm behind my back. His breath was hot and wet in my ear. "Make a peep," he whispered, "and I'll snap your arm like a twig off an apple tree."

Maybe they don't know Mom and Dad are gone. They can't take chances. My eyes swept around the bathroom, scouting for an escape, a plan, anything. The whole linen cabinet was emptied on the floor— towels, sheets, Ajax, shampoo, toothpaste, toilet paper, bath mats, and a nubby old heating pad. They'd removed two shelves, which were stacked against the vanity, and now I saw that Mattie was crouched inside the closet, moving a large magnet inch by inch across the wall. She was listening to the wall sounds with a doctor's stethoscope.

Why did I waste my time with a jelly jar? I wondered while Raymond kept his hand clasped over my mouth. I should have been afraid; these were dangerous people, and I was very vulnerable in my Thoreau nightshirt that barely reached midthigh. But, instead of fear, I was boiling over with rage. *How dare they do this to me!* I felt my eyes smoldering at the scene around me.

"Hold it. I think I hear something in here," Mattie said.

He had let up on my arm a bit, but now he tightened his grip again. "What did you find in our stuff, hunh, Ginger?"

I shook my head. *No, nothing.*

But Raymond didn't believe me. "Me and Mattie are taking you out for a little adventure, Ginger." He yanked on my hair. "Man, how I do hate red hair. Yup, a little moonlight river rafting. River's pretty high after all these storms, eh?"

His nails dug into my flesh. His other hand was flat against my lips. I worked my mouth open to catch a breath of air between his fingers and nearly heaved. I wanted to spit out the salty taste of his callused fingers. "Dad!" I yelled.

He cocked his head toward the door. "I don't hear anything, do you? When Mommy and Daddy stagger home and come in to see if Baby Ginger's breathing, why, they'll find just an empty bed."

He knew! I thought of that black river, water rolling, rolling.

Mattie backed out of the closet and signaled for Raymond to check out her finding. Her broad face towered over mine. She wore a fruity perfume that made it even harder for me to breathe. She handed Raymond a pillowcase.

He let go of my arm. I rubbed my throbbing shoulder and counted red nail tracks against the strained, bloodless white of my arm. But now he was snapping the pillowcase open. He meant to smother me! I backed toward the door, over the rubble, and slid down out of his grasp, like a greased pig.

Raymond whisked the pillowcase over my head. I sucked it into my mouth, tasting lint and cool air. One of them tore a strip from a sheet and tied it around my neck, while the other one stuffed a wad of something thick into my mouth. No more cool air. Dry, dry mouth. I could hardly swallow.

Dad! I screamed silently.

Chapter Twenty-Two
March 1857
NOT EVERYBODY GETS FREE

They reached Paducah on a Sunday. James had heard from the captain (who'd been checking on him several times a day after his "mad" spell) that Paducah was named for some words in the Chickasaw language that meant *place where wild grapes hang*. He smelled the sweet fruit and longed to lie down in a grape arbor and let those juicy, purple marbles drop into his mouth.

"We've got a greeting committee," Will pointed out.

On the shore hundreds of black people stood in silent clumps, some weeping, some waving kerchiefs, all watching something clattering down the road. James turned to get a better look. A black fiddler scratched out a mournful dirge on a violin badly in need of tuning. He led a solemn parade, a coffle of some forty or fifty men connected by short chains and all of them fastened to a long chain that draped between each two men. The clanging of those chains chilled James until he shivered, despite the hot Kentucky sun.

Behind the men in single file walked a smaller group of women, tied wrist-to-wrist. Some had babies scissored on their hips; some young children walked among the women. Each person in the coffle was barefooted. A line of guards watched their every step and shoved them back in line if they strayed even a few inches.

In horror, James asked, "Where are they going, Solomon?"

"Being sold down the river."

"Where to?"

"Mississippi, Tennessee, Alabama. Places where cotton grows. Miz Lizbet told me about it," he said bitterly. "It's Kentucky's pride to sell so many slaves South."

Will paced and sucked on sunflower seeds. "Well, why don't they put up a fight?"

Solomon gave him a sad stare. "Does it look to you like they've got a prayer of a chance? One falls, they all fall."

"They don't have to go like sheep."

"You, Mr. Will, you're a maverick. These folks have never had a chance to be anything but the flock herded by cruel overseers. But they do fight, sometimes. There are stories about men filing off their chains once they get on the boats and overthrowing some of the guards, but all it amounts to is a big stir. When all the bodies are counted, the rebels end up back in chains. Hunh-uh, this isn't the time to fight. You got to get to them when the odds are in their favor. You understand odds, Mr. Will. I saw you stacking up chips at the poker table. We got to play our cards right to get those folks free over in Owensboro."

Will nodded.

"So all these people are here to say good-bye to their friends?" asked James.

"Their husbands and fathers and sons. Those sisters tied together? Those are their daughters and wives. Owners, they don't care if a family gets busted up, the mother goes to a plantation in Alabama, the daddy stays in a hemp factory in Kentucky. To them it's no different from pulling away pups just been weaned."

James imagined Solomon, his *friend,* chained to a dozen other men and led barefooted away from the people he loved. James would be standing on the sidelines with his family and the Olneys, who were the closest folks Solomon had to a family, and even Miz Lizbet, all of them standing by and just letting this terrible thing happen. Well, Ma wouldn't have. He remembered her saying that nobody owns another human being. And yet these folks were being sold and shipped off like live-stock.

Solomon had the wall of his back to James, and James wasn't sure why. Was it grief? Shame? Anyway, he honored Solomon's privacy, until Will spit out a mouthful of sunflower husks and said gruffly, "Come on. We've got ninety miles to Owensboro."

First they had to repack, because they couldn't haul Ma's basket trunk all that distance. Most of the food was gone except for some chicory coffee and the hard biscuits and a bar of chocolate. James had pitched the clotted milk into the Missouri when it started smelling rancid.

They stuffed clothing and blankets and cups and a pan and the remaining odds and ends into pillow slips, and what flashed through James's mind was the image of those Eastern immigrants' possessions strewn all over the dock. Solomon and James each tied a pack to their back, but Solomon's was twice the size of James's. He regretted being such a runt when the job called for a strong back and broad shoulders.

Will still had his small rucksack, from which he pulled everything in the world he needed as if it were a magician's hat. Now he spread the map out before them. "Look here, we'll ford a shallow place across the Tennessee River, clip the top of Marshall County, cut across Livingston, shave the northeast tip of Caldwell, head north and east through Hopkins County, cross the Green River at Livermore, and then it's a straight shot north and east into Owensboro. Won't take us but four or five days if somebody with a wagon takes pity on us a time or two." He squinted at the sun, stuck a licked finger up to judge which way the wind was blowing, and led them to the McCracken-Livingston county line. "Trust me," he said. "I'm just as good as a Delaware Indian scout leading a man west to all that gold just waiting to be found."

Four or five days! *Impossible,* James thought. Why, he'd spent the first twelve years of his life in the comforts of Boston. He wasn't fit for tramping across Western terrain. But, on the other hand, Will seemed so sure of himself. Then again, Solomon tensed into a tight rope every time the eyes of a white man settled on him.

Maybe they should have just taken their chances on the *Francie Mulryan* and sailed all the way up the Ohio to Owensboro. No, too dangerous. Solomon had heard from some of the men and women on the boat that the deeper you got into Kentucky waters, the more dangerous it was for black folks. They'd just have to stay alert, as Pa had warned, and choose their friends carefully.

Will never seemed to tire. At night, when James and Solomon were ready to make camp and fry a fish or a rabbit Solomon had snared, Will wanted to forge on ahead. So Solomon enticed him to sit around the campfire with stories of slaves who'd made free.

"Sometimes people escape on steamboats just like the *Francie Mulryan*. There used to be a law in

North Carolina, over on the coast, that all vessels heading north, they'd be smoked out at the end of the trip."

"Why's that, Solomon?"

"Think about it, Mr. Will. You pump that boat with smoke after the passengers are out, and whoever's hiding in cargo or under a deck or in the boiler room, he'd suffocate, sure as the sun rises."

The fire crackled and sent sparks into the black night, and James fell into the rhythm of Solomon's story, so like Miz Lizbet's.

"Two men, their names were Abram Galloway and Richard Eden, they thought they'd outsmart those boat patrols. They made themselves hoods, or maybe gunnysacks, big enough to slip over their heads and shoulders, tying at the waist with a drawstring. They had them some gourds of water and towels. When the boat patrols were ready to smoke out the ship, Abram and Richard would press those wet towels to their noses and mouths so as not to burn out their lungs."

"They survived the smoke?" asked Will.

"Didn't have to. It turned out the boat never did get smoked out."

"Good," James said.

"What happened was worse. Richard and Abram, they stowed away in the cargo deck with barrels of turpentine. Ever breathe turpentine?"

"Sure, plenty, when my pa and I clean our guns," Will said.

"Out in the fresh air, you can breathe. Where these men were, it was close, hardly any air, and with every breath, they pulled in those turpentine fumes. It all but sucked the blood right out of them."

"But they made it, right?" Will asked impatiently.

"Well, sure they did. You think I'm going to tell you about the failures, Mr. Will? Soon as they swallowed some fresh Northern air, they were okay. Went on to Canada. Amen."

James chuckled. "You've been around Miz Lizbet Charles too long."

"Not long enough," Solomon said sadly.

They listened to the fire and the crickets awhile, until Solomon began again. "And talking about breathing, three other men, they tried their luck on a steamer. A black steward gave those men a hand. He was a slave himself, hired out to the steamship company by the owner. He hid the three in the boiler room. They had to lie down on the hot floor. There was barely room to move, no light, stingy bit of air, and blazing heat. They couldn't turn this way or that, for fear of frying their skin on the boilers that burned coal and wood to fuel the ship night and day. The whole trip they breathed nothing but coal dust, until their lungs rattled like they had gravel inside them."

Will asked, "You telling us they survived, too?"

"They did. Came out of that place in Philadelphia covered with coal dust. Only thing is," Solomon said, laughing, "it was raining hard that day, and the dust turned to a mud plaster on their faces and bodies. Just imagine how they must have looked."

"Bet they wanted a bath first thing," James said.

"Hunh-uh. Water, first thing, then some bread, and *then* a bath. Even an ox has got to eat and drink," Solomon said.

"You got any more stories?" asked Will.

"Hundreds. Miz Lizbet told 'em to me by the hour while we took each other through the fever. I heard a lot more on the *Francie Mulryan*. There's Miz Margaret Garner. She ran off from a plantation in Covington, Kentucky. Swore to kill all four of her children before she'd let them be taken back into slavery. She went to trial for one of the murders." Solomon stopped, and James knew he'd not tell another word of the story.

"So? Tell us what happened," Will urged.

"No, sir, I changed my mind, because it didn't have a happy ending for Miz Margaret Garner. Not everybody gets free and clear."

Chapter Twenty-Three
AIR!

Raymond Berk was still tapping the walls of the closet, but Mattie had me on the floor, up against the bathroom door, with her beefy leg flung over me and both my arms in her grip. Her thick strawberry perfume nearly made me heave.

I sucked the pillowcase in and out until it was soggy, but I couldn't expel the washcloth they'd jammed into my mouth. And then I heard, *"Squawk! Squawk! Brrrook!"* That was Firebird's protest when Dad threw the sheet over his cage each night. They were home!

I began thrashing around, throwing my head against the bathroom door, and Mattie didn't have enough hands to hold me still.

"Dana?" It was Dad's voice coming up the stairs.

Mattie froze and whispered, "Raymond, get out of the closet," but she didn't loosen her grip on me. I strained to hear Dad in the hall.

"What's going on in there, Dana? Sounds like you're trapping a wild animal."

"Mmmmn, mmmmn," I yelled from deep within my throat.

I heard Raymond back out of the closet and thrust the window sash up.

"What about me?" Mattie protested. "Leave me here holding the bag?"

Raymond must have had one leg over the windowsill when Dad rattled the doorknob. "Dana? You okay?"

"Uhhhhh!"

"Hold on, baby. I'll get the key."

The key box opened with such force that keys flew off their hooks and clattered against the wall.

Then I heard my mother bounding up the stairs. "Jeffrey? What's going on?"

"Dana's got trouble." A skeleton key clicked in the lock. Mattie's grip tightened around me as she thrust our combined weight against the door. But Dad and Mom had panic and adrenaline on their side, and they forced the door open.

Mattie let go of me, and I heard her clunk into the bathtub, cussing. Maybe she was on her way out the window when we both heard Raymond thud to the ground two stories below. A guttural growl told me he'd broken something in the fall.

"Oh, my God," Mom cried as she spotted the chaos in the bathroom. She ran to the phone in the hall while Dad untied the pillowcase around my head.

Air!

And there was Mattie Berk, trapped in the bathtub.

A policeman nabbed Raymond in his hound dog pajamas outside, where he was trying to camouflage himself in the bushes. The other officer, Detective Oberman, unwedged Mattie from the tub.

"This woman is a guest of yours, Dr. and Mrs. Shannon?"

"Not a friend guest, a paying guest. Our first," Mom replied. "Jeffrey, maybe we're not cut out for the bed-and-breakfast business."

Detective Oberman handcuffed Mattie and flipped open a little black notebook. "Name?"

"Mattie Berk," she said sourly.

The detective pulled a laminated card out of the back of the notebook and read in a monotone, "You have the right to remain silent . . ."

"Yeah, yeah, I know, I watch TV," Mattie growled.

Detective Oberman read the rest of the card, anyway, then said, "As you can imagine, Ms. Mattie Berk, you have a warm invitation to join us down at the station to stick your thumbs in some black ink and have your pictures made. Then we have a few dozen questions for you." She gave Mattie a shove out into the hall, hinting that the invitation wasn't optional.

Chapter Twenty-Four
March 1857
PROMISED LAND

The first night out, Will and Solomon and James camped at the head of Buck Creek in Livingston County. Solomon rigged up a fishing line and stuck a wriggler on the end of it, hoping one of those rainbow-coated trout would take the bait instead of just staring up at them with his sassy eye.

"Can't wait for trout," Will told them, balancing on his one leg. He had the empty leg of his trousers pinned up to his shirt to keep it out of the water. "You gotta go noodling." He crawled out of the creek and flattened himself on the bank. Creeping along on his elbows, he got right up close to the water and froze for such a long time that James considered feeling for a pulse. But he was alive, all right, scaring all of Solomon's trout away by staring back at them.

"What's 'noodling'?" James finally asked.

"Shh. Watch." There was the slightest movement under a branch sticking out over the water. Will inched forward, reached out in slow motion, and grabbed a big old snapping turtle, must have been three pounds. He held it up, with its legs flailing, and brought it to his face. "Howdy, Barleycorn!" The turtle pulled its head in, no more wanting to kiss Will than James did.

"Two more of these, and we've got a feast. My pa says these critters have got five flavors to them. Chicken, fish, pork, beef, and plain old turtle. You're in for a treat."

He plopped Barleycorn into the kettle, where the poor turtle clicked around until he decided to give up the fight.

They made Madisonville, the Hopkins County seat, the second night, and came upon a general store at the edge of town, where they bought a bottle of milk and two big pieces of gingerbread to split three ways. They slept under trees just bursting with new spring growth until sunrise, when the birds went crazy and the farmers came to town.

One of the farmers, noticing Will's one leg and crutch, said he'd be glad to take them as far as Nebo. The farmer gave Solomon a puzzled look, but he didn't ask any questions. Solomon wisely took a place in the back of the wagon without a fuss. The farmer gabbed the whole six miles and finally said, "This here's Nebo. Named for that mountain Moses stood on looking down into the promised land he didn't never get to."

That was one of the things in the Bible that

made James mad, though he didn't dare tell Ma. It sure wasn't fair that Moses spent forty years wandering with those stubborn, stiff-necked people who doubted him at every turn, and when the reward came at the end, Moses didn't get any of it. Of course, Ma would say Moses got his reward in the next world, but James wasn't sure Moses felt that way, watching those Israelites cross over the river Jordan, and him alone on the mountain.

"You ast me, Nebo's the promised land, right and true," the farmer was saying. "A real green land of Canaan here in the middle of the Western coalfields. Yessir, it's where I'm gonna be buried, and you can put money in the bank on that fact." He let them off and handed them each an ear of corn for the rest of their journey.

At Livermore, the Rough River and the Green poured together, and there was water as far as James could see, and platters of ice not yet thawed by the thin spring sun floating on the river.

"How we going to get across that?" Solomon asked. He was tired and irritable from their four days on foot, and James was reminded that Solomon had twenty-five years on Will and him. Will seemed to be the only one who never got tired, even with that one leg doing double time.

"Look." Will spotted the barges first. "We got money, we can hire a barge."

The bargeman appeared out of nowhere, palm out. "You got papers for this Nigra?"

Solomon stared at the ground as James answered, "Yes, sir, I do." This deep into Kentucky was no time to talk about free black men, so James produced the paper swearing that he was the son of a man named Bufford Bullock, scion of Daviess County, and Solomon was their manservant.

"Hemp, I reckon?"

"Miles and miles of it," Will said merrily.

"Makes mighty good rope and canvas and such. You another son?"

"Cousin, sir, from down in Looziana, Baton Rouge to be exact, on the Cranwoll side of the family."

James was afraid Will would get them into a knot they couldn't untie, so he quickly jumped in. "We've been doctoring up in St. Louis."

The bargeman eyed Will carefully, and as luck would have it, Will had a sudden attack of Phantom Limb and winced convincingly with the pain.

"Just healing, is it?"

"Fresh as new-killed deer," Will said, gasping.

"Well, I reckon you boys need this man here to see you home proper. Give my regards to Mr. Bullock. Tell him Scamp over in Livermore says howdy."

Suddenly James felt hot all over. "Thee knows . . . you know my pa?"

The bargeman grinned. "Not yet, I don't, but I'm not through living yet, either."

Sighing in relief, James and Will and Solomon settled onto the barge and within minutes were on the far bank of the Green River, with only a day's walk left into Owensboro.

Just outside of Panther, they saw a broadside nailed to an oak tree. In giant black letters, it advertised, NEGRO DOGS. Curious, James studied it more closely.

SPLENDID LOT OF WELL-BROKE NEGRO DOGS. WILL ATTEND ANY REASONABLE DISTANCE, TO THE CATCHING OF RUNAWAYS, AT THE LOWEST POSSIBLE RATES. ALL THOSE HAVING SLAVES IN THE WOODS WILL DO WELL TO ADDRESS W. D. GILBERT, OF FRANKLIN, SIMPSON COUNTY, KENTUCKY.

Solomon covered his eyes and walked away. Will said, "That's what we're up against, James. It ain't going to be easy."

After that, James got edgy and nearly fell in a creek when a measly squirrel scuttled across his path.

Will said, "You're as skittish as my ma when a mouse run over her foot."

"It's just that we're almost there, and we don't exactly have a plan," James said in self-defense.

"We do have a plan, Mr. James," Solomon said. "A piece of a plan, that is. Well, it's more like a sliver of a piece of a plan. Thing is, we don't know what's ahead. We don't even know how many people Miz Lizbet promised."

"Solomon's right, James. If we get tied down to a big, complicated plan, and we run into trouble, we're sunk. See that house over there with its porch leaning into the dirt? That's how sunk we'll be. Sunker."

Solomon patted James's back. "We'll be all right, Mr. James," he said, but he sounded like he needed convincing himself. He began singing one of the songs Miz Lizbet used to sing, about stealing away home to Jesus, and the song seemed to buck him up. Even his pace quickened.

"Flexibility, that's the ticket," Will shot back over his shoulder. "If there's one thing I learned riding with John Brown, it's keep your guard up, keep yourself loose, and be ready for battle any hour, day or night."

"That's three things," James said, trying to sound brave, but in his heart he worried that he'd be ready, all right, ready to run at the first sign of trouble.

Chapter Twenty-Five
THE FIRE-EATER

Dad made hot cocoa, and Mom hiked herself up on the kitchen counter by the fridge. "Well," she said, "our first bed-and-breakfast guests have come and gone, one of them out the window, I might add. It went well, don't you think, Jeffrey? They've destroyed our bathroom, terrorized our daughter, trampled our jonquils, gone to jail, and I've wasted two entire sour cream coffee cakes on them. This is *not* good for business, you understand."

Dad handed me a mug foaming with melted marshmallows. "What were they looking for, Dana?"

"James Weaver's drawings, I guess." I didn't believe my own words. The Berks were obviously after something much more valuable, something that mixed up James Weaver and the Delaware Indians. I *had* to find whatever it was they were looking for, but I didn't dare tell my parents yet. Parents get hysterical over the least little thing and start coming down on you with restrictions and warnings and groundings and other unreasonable responses.

Take the Renaissance Festival, for example. Last

fall we were reading *Julius Caesar* in English and Mrs. Flanaghan was making us do incredibly complex Shakespeare projects, and she made it clear that our going to the Renaissance Festival would put her in a better mood when she graded our projects.

So, one Saturday last fall, Mike's brother Howie drove a bunch of us to the festival. The way my parents carried on, you'd have thought we were going to Katmandu, instead of Bonner Springs, thirty miles away. Were there seat belts for everyone? Did we have rain gear? Hiking boots? Up-to-date maps? Water? Food and blankets in case the car broke down? A car phone? And don't eat the roasted pig—trichinosis, you know. And watch out for overzealous strangers. And did we know that pickpockets run rampant in a casual crowd like that? By the time they were done briefing and provisioning us, we were ready for a hike across the Himalayas.

The festival was amazing: Elizabethan dances and songs and foods and crafts; jousting knights and jugglers; men rattling around in chain mail; and women in dresses that made their chests come up to their chins. And there was a fire-eater.

Awed, I watched him put a flaming stick into his mouth, hold it there about ten seconds, and when he pulled it out, it was still on fire. Also, he still had a tongue. It didn't look that hard; *Mind over matter,* I thought. So when we finished our kebabs of beef and potatoes roasted over an open fire, that empty stick just called out to me.

Mike dared me: "Go ahead, Dana, do it."

Sally said, "Don't be stupid!"

"My uncle Pham eats fire," Ahn said. "But he has a tongue like a rope."

"Aw, she's too chicken to do it," Jeep taunted, waving the empty stick over the fire. It caught, like a match, like a piece of eager kindling, and I just popped that glowing sucker into my mouth.

"Ouch!!!" The fire went right out, but not before it fried the inside of my cheeks into cooked flaps of skin and wiped out a couple thousand taste buds. Even now, months later, I can't tell salty from sweet, but my tongue's coming back.

Sally whisked me right over to first aid, where they scolded me for about twenty minutes while I sucked on chipped ice. An hour later I could hardly talk, and Jeep felt so guilty that he bought a drink and gave me all the ice cubes, which left his Sprite as warm as bathwater.

Of course, my parents found out, mostly because I talked like a person with a mouthful of cotton when I got home, and they totally overreacted. If they'd had a tower, they'd have locked me in it, and since my curly hair bushes *out* instead of responding to gravity like Rapunzel's, I'd never have grown it long enough to make my escape.

So, obviously, only a few months after the Fire-

Eating Caper, I wasn't about to tell my parents how close I was to finding whatever it was Mattie and Raymond were so eager to tap our walls for. I'd have to wait for the right opportunity to finish their work, when my parents were both out.

Chapter Twenty-Six
March 1857
ONE GOES, WE ALL GO

Miz Lizbet had told Solomon that the safest time for strangers to appear on the plantation was Saturday night, when the work week was done and the field workers were dancing and cooking outside and carrying on like they were free as robins and Monday sunup seemed a long time off. Besides that, the overseers would be heady with their own merrymaking away from the slaves' quarters.

"That's the only time my mother, Pru, will be in a fit mood," Miz Lizbet had said. "You don't want to cross Miz Pru Biggers at her cranky time, amen."

Nearly two weeks after leaving Lawrence, they were finally approaching the spot Miz Lizbet had marked on the map. Kentuckians called it Yellow Bank, two miles south and west of Owensboro. Dark had settled on the bushy hedgerow that made a fence around the quarters, and a half-moon painted the leaves silver. James heard mandolin strumming and hushed singing that grew bolder as the moon rose.

Solomon whispered, "Mr. James, Mr. Will, I've got to go in alone."

"We didn't come this far to hide in the bushes," Will argued.

"They see you two fine-looking white boys, even scruffed up as you are, and they're going to run indoors quick as mice running into holes."

So James and Will crouched in the hedges and watched and listened.

By now a crowd had formed, and in the lantern light James saw men, women, and children dressed like they were going to a church supper, except they were all barefooted. The women had colorful striped kerchiefs wound around their heads, and the men wore red kerchiefs tied at their necks. What struck James most was the ringing laughter among the children, as if they were telling stories not meant for adults' ears. Everyone seemed to be in motion to the music. But when Solomon approached with his hat over his heart, all the music, singing, and dancing stopped at once, as if the conductor had snapped his baton down. Mothers pushed their little ones behind their skirts and hushed the bigger ones.

"Evening, folks. Name's Solomon Jefferson. I'm looking for Miz Pru Biggers."

A tall man stepped forward, his white shirt gleaming in the moonlight. His legs bowed like he'd just come off a horse, and his voice was deep and sure and left no doubt that *this* was the man in charge. "Ain't nobody here go by that name."

Solomon nodded knowingly. "Yes, sir, but somebody told me I could find her here."

"Who told you that?"

James watched Solomon take a deep breath before he said her name: "Miz Lizbet Charles sent me. She said some of you folks are waiting for her."

There was a stirring among the people, then a thin sapling of a woman elbowed her way out of the crowd. Her gray hair was wild and woolly, like a sheep needing shearing, and her bony finger pointed away from Solomon until someone gently turned her body toward him. "Why ain't she come herself?"

"Miz Pru?" Solomon stepped forward, and the old woman looked at him and around him at the same time.

"She's blind," James whispered to Will.

"That's news. We're gonna cover half the country with an old blind woman?"

"Shh, listen."

"Miz Pru, I bring you sad news. Miz Lizbet closed her eyes for the last time this past winter. The fever took her."

Someone murmured, "She done gone home to Jesus."

A couple of ladies stepped forward to support Miz Pru's elbows, but she shook them off. "Who're you?"

"Ma'am, I was fixing to marry your daughter, a fine woman."

Miz Pru's hand reached up for Solomon's face. He had to bend so she could run her bony fingers over his eyes, his nose, his lips, his stubbly cheeks. "You ain't no Matthew Luke Charles," she said, calling up the name of Miz Lizbet's dead husband.

"No, ma'am," Solomon agreed. "But I ain't no toad, neither." That brought soft chuckles from the crowd. "She sent me after you, Miz Pru."

The old woman thrust her shoulders back and stood all of five feet high, with wattles of flesh hanging from her arms. "Well, what took you so long? Look up at the sky." She tilted her head back as if she could see the points of light poking through the blackness. "You ought of come in the winter, like the song says. 'When the sun comes back and the first quail calls, follow the drinking gourd.' That's the winter, fool. That's when we s'pose to go, not after the spring done burst out and quail so thick, it's open season."

One of the women beside her said, "Let's hear what the man has to say. Come, sit down, Miz Pru. You've had a shock to the heart." She settled the old woman on a tree stump and came back to challenge Solomon. "I'm Sabetha. Say what you got to say, and say it quick."

Solomon nodded, and then he told them about James and Will. He explained how James's mother was a conductor on the Underground Railroad, and how Miz Lizbet had lived and died in James's house, and that impressed them some, but not half as much as hearing that Will had been with John Brown's men and lost a leg fighting slave catchers. And he told them that they'd all three come to finish Miz Lizbet's work.

Wary, the people hung back when James and Will came out of the bushes. Solomon said, "You can trust these boys, I swear on Miz Lizbet's soul."

"Ain't that stepping a little outta bounds?" The man who'd appointed himself leader stood nose-to-nose with Solomon, until Sabetha pushed him aside with the back of her hand and said, "This isn't your business, Jacob. Anybody ask you, you've seen and heard none of this. The rest of y'all best be blind, deaf, and dumb, too, hear?" She crooked her hand behind her, and a tall, lanky man with skin as dark as midnight stepped out of the crowd. His shoulders were rolled forward, and he carried a red rubber ball that he nervously passed, one hand on top of the other. Beside him was a girl who looked to be about ten.

Sabetha said, "This is Homer, and my girl, Callie. Me and Homer and Callie and Miz Pru are a family." Then she muttered, "Not one of 'em's my kin, except the girl." She stared defiantly at Solomon. "We're all set to go, four of us, just like Lizbet promised. One goes, we all go, hear?"

Chapter Twenty-Seven
ERNIE'S BAIT SHOP

The three of us went to Kansas City—Jeep, Mike, and I. Mike's brother Howie drove like a maniac, and he definitely needed to change the prescription on his glasses. *If we die on the road, my parents will kill me,* I thought.

Was Howie reading my mind? Squinting in the rearview mirror, he said, "I'm surprised your parents let you out of your cell for this trip."

"I didn't exactly tell them we were going all the way to Kansas City." I had the map spread out across my knees and was trying to make sense of all these suburbs and exits.

"Just don't swallow fire, and we'll be okay," Jeep warned me. "Hey, Howie, what did Mike have to pay you for this ride?" Howie *never* does anything for free. He's the kind of guy who'd charge an old lady for helping her across the street.

"You don't have to answer that," Mike said. He was riding shotgun in Howie's rattletrap Toyota. Most of the stuffing is out of the seat, and the gutted radio hangs by wires. The carpeting in the backrest looks like it's been through a shredder.

"Nice car," Jeep muttered.

Howie changed lanes for no apparent reason. "No, I'd like to answer it, Mike. It shows how desperate you are in front of your little buddies." He beeped his clown-nose horn as he swerved around a motorcycle. "I'm getting half his allowance for the next six weeks."

"You're tough," said Jeep. His fingertips were six shades lighter than his fingers as he pressed his hand into the roof of the car to keep from being tossed around.

"I look at it this way." *Beep-beep.* "In another eighteen months, Mike will have his learner's permit and he'll be unleashed on the public roads, so I've got to turn a profit while I can."

"Our exit's coming up."

"Which exit, Dana? I've got to cut in front of a truck, and those suckers don't stop on a dime."

"Slow down. Slow down!" I yelled. "Oops, you missed the exit."

Howie let loose of a few words that would cost me fifty cents each if they had escaped my lips in the presence of my parents. I was already three dollars in debt to them for similar blips.

At the next exit Howie spun a U-turn that reversed polarity, and we were heading back in the right direction. About ten minutes later we pulled up in front of a misshapen building that had curling shake shingles pocked with bird droppings. The windows were crossed out by large wooden *X*s nailed over them, and a faded sign hung lopsided over the barred door.

Ernie's Bait Shop sat right at the junction of the Kansas River and the Missouri River, but it looked as if it hadn't been open for business since the days of manual typewriters.

Chapter Twenty-Eight
March 1857
WICKED WICKER

The big problem was, how were they going to get Callie out in the middle of the night? Even though Sabetha was a house servant, at nine o'clock she was sent down to the quarters, where she slept with Miz Pru. Homer, who was Miz Pru's son, was mentally slow and needed looking after, so he unfurled his bedroll each night in Miz Pru's cabin as well. But Callie slept in the big house, curled up at the foot of Miss Amelia Bullock's bed. Miss Amelia was seven years old and scared of every creak of the house and every cry of the wind. Bad dreams chased her through most nights, and when she stirred, Callie, like a vigilant watchdog, sat up and reassured her that everything was just the way it was supposed to be. Callie had told James, "I sure don't sleep long, but I sleep real often."

So, how were they to get Callie out when they were ready to make their escape come Tuesday night when the moon was barely a slice in the night sky?

Solomon had a daring plan, which he worked out with Sabetha. That evening James cleaned up as sharp as he could and presented himself at Mr. Bufford Bullock's front door. William, a light-skinned butler, showed James into Mr. Bullock's back parlor, not the front one for distinguished guests. William said, "Mr. Bullock, sir, this here's young Mr. James Weaver wants to talk to you, sir."

James and Mr. Bullock nodded to each other. Mrs. Bullock's chair was back-to-back with her husband's so they could share a lamp, and she read through spectacles perched on the end of her arrow-sharp nose. She had her hair done up on top of her head, with chopsticks crisscrossed through her bun.

James glanced up at Sabetha, stationed along one wall sewing and pretending she'd never seen James once in her life.

This was the most beautiful room James had ever been in. The walls were burnished walnut, grain matched perfectly, and one wall was filled with books from the floor to the ceiling. The books were stacked every which way, as if people actually read them. When James followed the rainbows on the wall, he looked up to a crystal chandelier that dazzled him with its prisms of dancing light.

"Young James, what can I do for you?" Mr. Bullock put down the thick tome he'd been reading. Tufts of gray hair at each cheek only made his bald head and apple red cheeks all the more absurd. His eyes were the color of well water, and now they fell on James. "Young James?"

Sabetha pulled her sewing up to her face and glared at him over the top of it. James swallowed dry spit. "Sir, I'm on my way to New Orleans. Thee, uh, the reason is I've been to a doctor in St. Louis. I get terrible headaches, sir, make me see double until I think my head's going to explode."

"I presume the doctor helped you?"

"Oh, yes, sir. He gave me a powder to take, and I've been well since."

"I declare," Mrs. Bullock said in her tinkly voice. "I guess the New Orleans doctors haven't cottoned to that cure yet."

Mr. Bullock looked annoyed at his wife's interruption, and he asked, "You're not traveling all alone, are you, son?"

James saw Sabetha's warning, but he made a snap decision because it didn't figure that a rich New Orleans landowner would let his boy travel four hundred miles alone. "Oh, no, sir. My father sent one of our slaves with me, a trusted servant named S-Simon."

"And where is this Simon now, son?"

"Well, sir, he's taking bed and board with some distant kinfolk down in the quarters. They've given him a pallet on the floor."

"Southern hospitality. Very good," Mrs. Bullock said, "and you'll stay with us, James Weaver."

"Oh, I couldn't impose, ma'am."

"Nonsense. A refined gentleman such as

yourself doesn't travel by night like darkies on the run." She folded her glasses and stuck them in a hidden pocket on her lap. "Sabetha, see about arranging a room for young Mr. Weaver, and have the kitchen people bring him out some refreshment. Cold lemonade, James, wouldn't that be just the nicest little treat?"

"Thank you kindly, ma'am. I believe I can taste it already." And he could. It seemed like eons since he'd had anything so fresh and cold and sweet and tart as lemonade. Just the thought made the sides of his neck prickle with anticipation.

The Bullocks had fallen right into the scheme! "Well, sir, I'll just direct Simon to bring in my things."

"No need, son. William will take care of everything." Sabetha returned with the tray of lemonade, and with the parlor door open, James heard the men grunting in the hall as they carried in a huge wicker basket filled with hay and stones.

A few minutes later, Mrs. Bullock tapped her mouth delicately to hide a yawn. "I do believe it's time to turn in."

James jumped to his feet. "Oh, yes, ma'am, a day of traveling takes the wind right out of me." He nodded to Mr. Bullock and followed Mrs. Bullock upstairs, where she pointed out his room and the nearest water closet and detoured to her daughter's bedroom. "Before I go to bed, I always listen at her chest to be sure the sweet thing's breathing. She's such a fragile little flower, don't you know."

James also knew Callie would be curled at the foot of the bed, eyes closed, waiting.

Once Mrs. Bullock was behind her own closed door, Sabetha appeared out of nowhere, hissing last-minute instructions to James before she left for her cabin. "Callie's ready. Miz Pru and Homer and me, we've got our traveling needs all packed up. Homer's saying good-bye to the dogs. That could take half the night," she muttered.

Mrs. Bullock poked her head out of her room at the end of the hall, and Sabetha darted into James's room. "You need anything, James, just ring, heah? There's servants answer the bell anytime, night or day."

"Thank you, Mrs. Bullock," James called back.

Behind him, Sabetha whispered harshly, "You know what to say if they catch you. Don't you mess this up, Northern Boy."

The next time Miss Amelia woke up, Callie gave her one of Miz Pru's healing teas, made of gander root and gallweed, and Miss Amelia sank into a sleep that wouldn't lift until dinnertime next day, if then. The doctor would be called, and in all the confusion maybe no one would attend to the disruption in the household.

Once Miss Amelia was snoring, Callie tapped on James's door. "She's out like a drunken soldier." Solomon came out of the closet, which was now stuffed full of hay and stones. He pulled the emptied wicker basket behind him, and Callie climbed in. Her eyes were tough, but her voice was pleading: "I ain't got much flesh on my bones. Don't you be bouncing me around like I'm nothing but an old tire."

They started down the stairs with the basket. Callie was a lot heavier than she looked standing upright. Not much flesh? Then she must have had mighty heavy bones. James noticed the light in the back parlor, which meant they dared not go out the back way as planned. They tiptoed through the front hall, where the floorboards creaked their alarm.

Mr. Bullock came out of the parlor. "Where you going with that traveling basket, young James?"

No need to introduce Solomon. James knew he'd be invisible to Mr. Bullock. "I figure on getting an early start tomorrow morning, sir, so's I can make New Orleans by dark. I thought while my man Simon was handy, we'd just get my trunk outside so we wouldn't have to disturb anybody in the morning bustle. It'll be all right out here on the porch, I reckon."

"I expect. You sure don't travel light, son." Mr. Bullock worked the clasp of the basket. "What have you got in here, half my stone quarry?" He started to lift the lid!

James let out a bloodcurdling howl. "Oh, my headache's come back something fearsome." He grabbed both sides of his head and rocked it, his eyes wide and wild, his lips quivering. "Owie-yowie-yow! I'm good as dead, oh, help me, Lord!"

Mr. Bullock dropped the lid of the basket and led James to the front parlor, where he lowered him onto a puffy brocade settee. He pulled a bell cord, and William appeared. "Get young Mr. James a cool, wet cloth, William."

James kept his face twisted as if the pain were doing him in. He let his eyes flutter helplessly as he moaned and groaned, ever louder, while Solomon slid the basket out the front door.

Chapter Twenty-Nine
TONGANOXIE

Jeep and I peered in the window while Mike circled the building and Howie stayed in the car munching Chee-tos and reading Pat Conroy's *The Lords of Discipline*. Mike said he'd been reading it for two years and about ten thousand bags of Chee-tos.

"I don't see much in there, do you, Jeep?"

"Just some rusty hooks and a few lures and bobs. A lot of dead stuff on the floor. The birds have found heaven, that's for sure."

Suddenly something moved, and we heard a shriek: "Ernie! Ernie!"

"Who's that?"

Jeep cupped his eyes against the glare of the window. "Hey, it's a parrot."

"Ernie! Ernie!" the bird squawked, flying from one light fixture to another. His wings were a neon green, and a tuft of orange bisected his eyes.

"Looks like a punk rocker," said Jeep. "He's staring at us like we're his lunch."

"But he's lively. Somebody's been feeding him." The parrot was three times the size of Firebird and much noisier, screeching and cackling in sounds Firebird hadn't discovered yet.

Then a piece of the floor rose up, and a man's head poked out of the hole. He grew taller as he climbed the hidden stairs under the trapdoor. The parrot went berserk.

"Ernie! Ernie! Lover boy! Lover boy!" He fluttered over and landed on the man's head, with his beak pecking at one eyebrow.

"Must be feeding time at the zoo," Jeep said.

"And it must be Ernie. Duck, before he sees us."

We squatted out of sight and heard Ernie talking, as if that parrot were his best friend *and* deaf. "Come here, Tonganoxie," he bellowed. "Here pretty-pretty bird. That's my boy."

I darted up for a quick peek. I recognized Ernie. "Jeep," I whispered, "it's the man who was prowling around my yard."

The bird was perched on Ernie's thumb, and they were nose-to-beak. "You've got to see this, Jeep. They're kissing."

Jeep popped up. "Oh, gross. Wait till Sally hears about this."

We crouched down again, and when we dared to peek once more, Ernie had vanished and the bird was right at the window.

Mike scared us to death coming up right behind us. "I've made a full-circle inspection of the building. Everything's padlocked, and all the locks are rusted. Nobody's been in or out of here in ages."

"Except the guy inside," Jeep said.

"Ernie. I guess he lives under the shop." I gazed down the road at a shack that slouched against the sky about thirty feet away. "That's some tunnel from here to there. Maybe this was a stop on the Underground Railroad. Tunnels, trapdoors—it fits the picture."

Jeep agreed. "Hey, Mike, another thing that couldn't possibly be in the bait shop is the parrot that's inside. Ernie's in love with him. Wanna see him? His name's Tonganoxie."

"That's a weird name for a bird," Mike said. "I've heard it somewhere before."

I knew a town by that name. "We drove through it last summer. There's a big old statue of Chief Tonganoxie in the center of the town, and that's about all there is to the place."

"Chief of what?" Jeep asked.

I caught my breath. "You know what, guys? He was a Delaware Indian chief right around Miz Lizbet's time."

"And those Berk people had an old Delaware book, right? Bingo." Jeep ran his hand over his shaved head, which sounded rough as sandpaper. "I say let's start fitting the pieces together."

"And I say let's get Howie in gear again and look for more pieces at the Berks' house."

"Wait a minute," Mike said. "We're not going to break in."

"No, of course not!" I protested, wondering if I could use my Blockbuster Video card to trip the lock on their door.

We took one more peek in the window. Tonganoxie's licorice-dot eyes stared right at us.

Mike shuddered. "The bird gives me the creeps."

Tonganoxie's beak opened: "Pretty-pretty bird!"

"Oh, shut up," Mike growled.

Chapter Thirty
March 1857
THE CRUNCH OF FOOTSTEPS

Midnight. Escape night. James and Will waited at the end of the road for the first sign of someone's head above the hedges. A few advance-guard crickets chirped farewell wishes, but the night held an eerie stillness. Every footstep would be detected.

Worms crawled around in James's belly. He took a deep breath to quiet them, while Will tapped the earth with his crutch.

"What's taking them so long, James? Gol, half the night's gone."

Then here came Homer, pulling Miz Pru along with him. She looked all misshapen and spiky, loose parts barely held together by a rope cinching her waist.

"Mama Pru done got hemp stalks and turkey feathers stuffed all 'bout her," Homer whispered. "Somebody shoot her, it don't go through. My idea," Homer boasted. "I ain't stupid, no, suh."

"Itches like wool underdrawers," Miz Pru grumbled.

Callie came out next, quiet as a rabbit in the

bush. She asked, "Is this gonna work? We really gonna be free tomorrow?"

"It'll take a few weeks," Will explained. "The first couple hours of daylight will be the most dangerous. Are you brave, girl?"

"Brave as any one-legged boy," she huffed.

In a few minutes Sabetha was out. "You're all standing here like it's the county fair. Be going!"

"As soon as Solomon comes," James said, but Will was already leading the others through a path he'd scouted deeper into the forest.

At last Solomon appeared. "I had to argue with that stubborn Jacob, tell him he couldn't come this time because we've already got a whole army marching with us. He's got to cover for us back there." Solomon had the jitters.

"You all right?" James asked, as much to settle the worms in his own stomach as to ask after Solomon.

"Been better," he said.

The seven met in the dark of the forest for last-minute instructions. Calmer now, Solomon said, "There's no light but the moonlight. We can't light fires because they draw attention. Another thing: We can't travel like a pack of wolves."

"If you're thinking about leaving me behind, think on it again, boy," Miz Pru said.

"No, ma'am. But once we get deeper into the trees, we've got to spread out. You'll come with

Sabetha and me. One of us is going to hold on to that rope hanging from your waist every minute, ma'am, so you can give it a tug or we can, to make sure we're safe on both ends. Does that sit with you all right, Miz Pru?"

"Time bein'," she conceded.

"Callie, you go with the boys, because the three of you have a better chance of outrunning those wretches they'll send after us."

Homer said, "I know where I be."

"Behind us all," Solomon confirmed.

"Yes, suh!"

While waiting all winter for Miz Lizbet to come back for them all, Miz Pru had fixed it so that Homer could take care of the Bullocks' bloodhounds. He had a way with dogs, and *she* had a way with the Bullocks. She explained that she was what they called a conjurer. She could do magic: make flowers grow, make fevers break. She knew herbs and roots and secret spells. More than once the Bullocks had called on her when one of the house Negroes had fainting spells or bothersome rashes, and she had nursed Mr. Bullock through a bout of food poisoning that had nearly sent him into the sweet hereafter.

So when she'd prevailed on Mr. Bullock to let her poor feeble son, Homer, tend the dogs, he had agreed. The hounds got so used to Homer's scent and him feeding and watering them that they would never betray him.

"When they send the bloodhounds sniffing after us," Miz Pru had explained, "my Homer, here, he gonna put them off our scent, you watch and see if it ain't so."

James prayed it *was* so, because he remembered Miz Lizbet telling him how those bloodhounds were bred to rip runaways to shreds on scent alone and didn't stop to wonder if the victim had black skin or white.

Now Sabetha drew her shawl around her shoulders and said, "You be careful, Homer, hear?"

"You betcha, Honey Sabetha. Those pups, they's mush in my hands. I ain't lettin' them near you or Mama Pru or Callie Girl."

Sabetha rose on tiptoes to kiss Homer's cheek, then hurried to catch up with Solomon and Miz Pru.

The night grew colder. James was grateful for his warm coat and boots, but Callie went barefooted.

Will asked, "How far you reckon you're going to get without shoes?"

She retorted, "How far you reckon you're going to get on one foot?"

"All the way," Will said.

"Same as you."

They trudged through fall leaves turned musky and soft in the spring rains, over thorny twigs and stones and rooted hillocks. Callie never complained; her feet were like tanned leather.

Something howled—a coyote? a wolf?—and

141

James's heart catapulted into his throat. Stars appeared and disappeared through the trees. In each clearing they searched for their reassuring marker in the sky, the North Star. If they kept in mind where they were in relation to the North Star, they'd be going the right way.

If the bloodhounds and slave catchers and bounty hunters and thin ice and bolts of lightning and wolf traps and hungry wolves didn't get them first.

They heard the crunch of footsteps ahead of them, although James could no longer see Solomon and the two women. They also heard Homer's plodding steps behind them as he hummed the same tune over and over.

James asked Callie, "Is Homer thy father?"

"Him? Nah. He's not even my mother's sweet-heart. We just look after him because he's Miz Pru's boy. Well, I s'pose he's a grown man. Anyway, my mama owes Miz Pru because she's teaching me the art."

"What art's that?" asked Will, who was using his crutch to part overhanging branches.

"Conjurer's art. She says it's a gift you gotta be born having. I say, chicken livers, you can learn it just like white men learn their doctoring. Why you think I wear this snakeskin around my neck, hmn? Because it's magic." Whipping around to show James and Will her snakeskin in a spot of moonlight, she tripped and tumbled over a felled log.

"That was pure magic," Will said.

Callie got up and brushed twigs and bugs off her cotton shift. Her legs were bare, caked and milky with traveling dirt. She waved each hand and foot in the air. "I didn't break anything. That's the magic part."

The tops of the trees were tinted in the lavender light of dawn. James said, "I guess thee noticed, Callie, Will doesn't ever get tired, but I'm ready to drop. I say we stop here for a couple of hours." In fact, it had been twenty-four hours since he'd slept, and his head felt like Ma's butter churn—round and hollow, with something pounding away in it. Sleep, that's all he wanted. And some food. A big slab of roasted beef sure would taste good, or some of Ma's bread hot from the oven, the kind that soaked up butter until it was limp in the middle and crunchy at the edges.

"This spot's okay," Will allowed. They were beside a stream swollen with spring rain, and they gobbled the clear, cold water by the handful. James splashed more of it on his face, to wake himself up. Callie took out a gingham napkin full of oatmeal bread, which wasn't exactly one of Ma's light-as-a-cloud loaves, but it felt good going down into the empty well of James's stomach. They each ate a tart green apple, and James was reaching for another one when Will said, "What little bit of food we could carry has got to last us a few more days until we get across the Ohio. Over in Indiana we'll probably find a safe house to spend a day in, and if we're lucky, we'll have us a proper hot meal."

Callie grudgingly retied the remaining food. Suddenly they heard Homer's mournful lowing, like an owl's hoot, meaning that the bloodhounds had found him.

"Oh, Law," Callie said. "You hear that?" The hounds were yipping and growling like somebody was beating them with a stick, but when the noise simmered down, what they heard was Homer lullabying the dogs.

They listened, barely breathing. "Whoa, Hannibal, you jes' hol' yo' fire. Down Mac, good dawg, good dawg. Pfft, pfft, here Daisy, tha's my girl, tha's my Daisy girl. Y'all jes' turn aroun' an' go back, like I done taught you. I ain't stupid, no, suh!"

If all went right, Homer would scramble up a high tree, and the dogs would turn back with their tails between their legs before the men caught up.

But that's not what happened. Homer and the hounds were cooing back and forth when suddenly Homer hooted again: The dogs had decided to push forward! James saw the first one loping through the trees. He was a yellow brown, lean hound with sleek legs and his nose to the ground, all business. James nudged Will, who stood frozen for just a second, until Callie pushed both the boys into the frigid water and jumped in herself, holding on to Will's crutch to keep herself afloat.

They scampered to the shore on the other side of the stream. In their sodden clothes, they rolled on the prickly ground behind some bushes. Teeth chattering, they watched the hounds anxiously trotting this way and that in frustration, on the bank across the stream.

Will grabbed his crutch away from Callie. "Why'd you do that? You lost us all our food." *And my sketchbook,* James thought mournfully.

"Oh, hush. It was the only way to wash off our scent so the dogs would lose us. Look, they've turned tail."

When the dogs' rear ends were just brown circles in the distance, Callie said, "What're those poor hounds gonna tell their sweethearts tonight standing around the supper bowl? That they were outfoxed by three chicken-livered young 'uns and an old half-wit?" Then she suddenly turned serious. "What do you s'pose happened to Homer?"

James imagined the worst, and even worse, having to tell Miz Pru when they caught up with her, but then Homer appeared on the opposite side of the stream, and Callie just about burst with joy. "Psst, over here," she hissed.

Homer didn't think to walk on the logs that bridged the stream. He just stuck his rubber ball between his teeth, jumped right in, and dog-paddled toward Callie's smiley voice.

Chapter Thirty-One
FLAT AS A COCKROACH

"At least we know the Berks won't be home," Jeep said as Howie pulled up to their house, "since they're taking room and board at the Douglas County Jail."

Howie snarled his warning: "If there's any trouble here, you'll pay. I'm talking police, the media, irate neighbors, rabid dogs, or anything else that falls into the category of unusual. Anything happens, and you all owe me half of your allowance for the next six weeks. I'll be in the car." I swear, if it had a toilet, Howie could live in that car around the clock. His girlfriend, Franny, probably cooks him meals on a hot plate plugged into the cigarette lighter.

The Berks' house looks just like all the others on the block: split-level, vintage 1950s, detached garage, chain-link fence—and a large, vicious-looking dog running loose in the yard, with a bark that sounded like he should be singing bass in the school chorus.

"That's it, I'm out of here," Mike said. "That's the kind of dog that goes right for the crotch, and

I'm planning to leave here with all the parts I came with."

But Jeep had already sweet-talked the dog and was inside the gate scratching his ears. The water bowl was dry, so Jeep found a tap in the yard and refilled the water. The dog lapped it up eagerly while Mike and I slipped past him to the front door.

"We're not breaking a lock or a window," Mike reminded me.

"No, but it can't hurt to see if they left something unlocked by accident. It's not breaking and entering if you knock loud, and no one answers, and you turn a doorknob, and it just happens to be open, and you step inside to see if anybody's home."

"In the movies, this is about the time you walk in and find a dead body on the floor."

"Don't get hysterical, Mike."

"I don't know how I get myself into these messes. It's you. You spread crisis wherever you go."

"That's what makes me an exciting woman." I remembered my mother telling Warren, my big brother who lives in Memphis, "Don't marry a boring woman. What could be worse than being bored to death?" Well, if her theory is accurate, with my track record I'll have lots of marriage proposals to turn down, because I'm not planning to get married for at least twenty-five years. Marriage is for old people, like my parents.

We rattled every doorknob and window. Everything was locked tight, and every drape and curtain closed. I couldn't even tell if the Berks had left a light on inside. "They sure are secretive people."

"Or careful people. You don't go out of town and leave your house open to the world." Mike tugged at my arm. "Let's go. There's nothing to see here."

"Wait, the garage." But the garage door wouldn't budge an inch.

"Satisfied?"

"No, I'm not. Jeep, over here."

Jeep came up on the porch, with the dog brushing against his jeans as if they were old buddies.

"Everything's closed up," I pointed out. "What do we do now? You're the expert. You're the one who got us into Wolcott Castle when it was all locked up."

"Yeah, and nearly killed myself falling through the balcony."

"But I saved you," I boasted. *That* would have to go on my marriage résumé, too.

Jeep asked, "Did you check the basement windows?"

"None of them open."

"This is stupid," Mike said. I was amazed at what a coward he was turning out to be. "Let's get out of here."

"Wait." The Berks' dog seemed to want to join in the search, and he began sniffing around as though he were on the tracks of some big game. So we followed him to the back of the house, where he showed us the flap door for a cat. I wondered if they'd had those in James Weaver's day, if he'd put a cat door in Wolcott Castle or any of the other fancy homes he'd designed. "Mike?"

"Don't look at me—I can't flatten myself like a cockroach and crawl through that space," Mike said.

"No, but Jeep could poke his head in, since he's got no hair to get tangled in the hinges. Here, let me hold your glasses so they don't fall off inside."

"Then how would I see what's in there?" Jeep stuck his head in the cat door.

"What do you see?" Mike asked.

"A green vinyl floor with a bunch of laundry all over it, and a cat dish, a litter box, and a broom and dustpan. Nothing special." His voice came back faint and hollow, until he yelled, "No! My glasses fell off." He pulled his head out of the door and stuck his arm in up to his shoulder, since his head and arm couldn't both fit at once. Groping around blind for his glasses, he came up with a handful of Kitty Litter. He yanked his arm out. "Next time do this stuff without me, hear?" He had to go back in and retrieve his glasses, but this time Mike held the flap open and directed his robot arm.

The dog began barking some sort of warning signal, so we went around to the front of the house to see what had agitated him. A woman stood in the front yard in a flowing purple dress dotted with paint.

One look at us, and she grabbed the whistle hanging around her neck and blew a wail that would wake hibernating bears. Instinctively all three of us flattened ourselves on the ground as if bullets were flying.

Chapter Thirty-Two
March 1857
THE OLD MAN IS A·WAITING

The surging Ohio River spread out before them, black and roaring and impossible to cross. Homer's eyes were as wide as silver dollars. "You see 'em over there? See my mama and Solomon and Sabetha Girl?"

Callie stared off into the void. "They're over there, all right."

James squinted and pretended he could actually spot them clear across the river. "Might be them," he assured Homer, but if they'd made it across, how in tarnation had they done it?

Or they could have been caught, tied up, hauled halfway back to Owensboro by now.

Or they could be dead. James's stomach rolled up to his throat at that thought. "No. No!"

"No what?" Callie demanded, still gazing across the unforgiving river.

"No . . . time to worry about it. Let's go," James said. He whistled for Will, who hopped out from behind some bushes, hitching up his trousers.

A luxurious steamboat side-paddled its way

through the center of the river, lights dancing on the water. James yearned to be on that boat just for one warm, dry, belly-filling night, but that wasn't possible, not with two escaping Negroes.

They walked upriver until they found a narrow crossing place. James said, "Reckon we can ford the river here? We can wade out to those melting ice islands." He remembered Miz Lizbet's tales of runaways crossing the river by leaping from one ice pocket to the next as if they were cobblestones.

"I don't know," Will said. "If any one of those floes out in the middle won't hold us, we'll sure enough drown in the icy water."

James reminded him that whatever ice wasn't broken up and melted by the steamboat would certainly be solid enough to support them.

"That water look mighty col'," Homer said, shaking his head. He tossed his rubber ball from hand to hand. "Freezin' mighty col'."

Callie was skeptical as well. "You expect me to jump from one piece of ice to another? Did you stop to think how my feet are going to freeze right onto that ice?"

But Homer had a solution. He pulled out of his shirt the gingham napkins that had once held his food, and he tied them around Callie's feet with perky little knots poking over the top. "Now you got red-and-white shoes, yes, suh!"

Homer and James, wearing boots, had no trouble leaping across the first three chunks of ice, and Callie followed them, slipping dangerously, but she was agile.

However, it was impossible for Will's crutch to gain purchase on the slick ice, and plumb hazardous for him to swing from one floe to another on his leg. And all this in the dark. "I can't do it," Will said grimly. "Y'all will have to go on without me."

James reached across and grabbed Homer's arm just as he was ready to jump to the next platter of ice. "We have to go back, all of us."

By the time they were back on the shore, Will had a better idea.

"In the first light we'll build us a raft."

James thought about the first runaway Ma had harbored at their house. He'd been a master with a hammer and nails; where was he *now?* Anyway, they had no tools to build a watertight raft that would carry them across this mean water.

Will had it all thought out, in spite of a cold rain that suddenly turned the morning into pure misery. He showed them how to build two makeshift rafts of logs and branches tied together with hickory withes. Then they had to wait the day out until it was safe to put their rafts into the chilly water.

Pelted with rain, they kept their eyes on the

flickering lanterns dotting the other side of the river and tried poling themselves across. Homer hand-paddled until his arms hung limp as flags, and all they did in their hours of labor was go round and round in ever-widening circles to avoid those same ice floes that were meant to be their salvation.

"We're through with this foolishness," Will announced. "I say we take our chances finding the fishermen Solomon heard about. He believes they're friendly, that they'll ferry us across in a skiff like they do others."

"But what if they're not friendly?" Callie argued. Her voice from the other raft seemed to bubble up out of the black water, for James couldn't see her at all. "They might just send us back to Bullocks'."

"No, suh, I ain't goin' back," Homer said, and he paddled even harder.

"Now's a good time for some of your magic, Callie," muttered Will. "Follow me, we're going back to shore."

They spread out on the shore. Tired as a racehorse, James gazed up at the heavens. The rain had let up a bit, and now he could see the North Star, taunting him, telling him that he and Callie and Will and Homer weren't any closer to the safety of Lawrence, Kansas, than they were to the stars themselves.

"What do you think about those fishermen they

said would help us?" Callie whispered, propped up on one elbow. She bolted up, and her elbow jabbed James. Her face was silvery in the moonlight. She closed her eyes, and James saw them working under her eyelids, like Ma in prayer. But Callie conjured up a different kind of miracle. Shivering and dozing, James heard her firm voice: "It'll be all right with the fishermen. I saw 'em."

"How'd thee see them, Callie? Tell me that."

"Mama Pru and me, we can see things before and after, we can see things up close and way far off. We can see what ain't even ever going to *be*."

Sometimes Ma said when she was praying that she could see things other folks missed because their minds were overgrown with weeds. But this was different.

James gave Callie a skeptical glance, and she bristled. "You don't have to believe me, James Weaver, but you'll see soon enough. The fishermen are waiting for us to come, and we gotta go *now*."

"Yes, suh!" Homer said as Callie pulled each of them to their feet. She barely said another word the rest of the night while they trekked on toward the fishermen's shack on rain-soaked ground as soft as a belly.

"That must be it," Will said, pointing to a small lean-to on the south bank of the Ohio. That place sure looked pitiful in the first light of morning, all rotted wood and nailed-up windows and a porch step sloping about forty-five degrees toward the ground.

Homer said, "Look like it'll fall over if the win' blow too hard."

Will studied Miz Lizbet's hand-drawn map. "Yep, right halfway between Owensboro, Kentucky, and Rockport, Indiana. That's the fishermen's hut, all right."

It had better be, James thought, because he couldn't bear one more night outside in the biting rain. Why hadn't somebody told Ma, when she came up with this harebrained idea, that March was the rainy season in these parts? Four days had passed since James had been dry, and his soggy stockings had worn blisters on his heels; every step was torture. The first two nights they'd been walking, James had passed the time by daydreaming about crisp white sheets and a big old heavy goose-down quilt such as Ma was always sewing on. The last two nights he'd dreamed about a hearty meal. By then they were eating nothing but the roots and berries and leaves Callie had learned about from Miz Pru, and an occasional scrawny carrot or potato they might pull up in somebody's garden that had barely taken root this early in the spring.

A thick rope of smoke twirled out of the chimney

of the fishermen's shack, promising warmth inside, maybe even some hot chicory coffee or steaming soup.

"I'd best go up to the door alone," James suggested. "Thee hide back until I'm sure Callie's prediction is right."

"Oh, chicken livers, James. I've seen these fishermen in my head. Just trust me."

"Thee doesn't know much about my family, Callie. My pa's a lawyer. With him, everything's got to be proved."

Callie crossed her skinny arms over her skinny chest. "Well, seems to me what you need's a little faith, James."

"Oh, I know about that, too," James said with a shimmering sigh. "My ma's one hundred percent faith. Faith and fortitude."

Will chuckled. "My ma says yours is the stubbornest woman she *ever* met."

"If your daddy's all proving, and your mama's all believing, it's a wonder they ever got together," Callie sputtered. "Go and knock on that door, Mr. Proofman, and you'll see I'm right."

No one answered. James pushed the door open a couple of inches; Callie crept up right behind him. The warmth of the room urged them forward—the smoldering embers in the fireplace and the black kettle swinging over the hearth, licked by little tongues of flame.

On the rough-hewn table was a message, burned into smooth hide:

WELCOME WAYFARERS. THE OLD MAN IS A-WAITING.

"What does thee suppose that means, the old man¿"

"It's the song, James, doesn't anybody sing it where you come from¿ 'The old man is a-waiting for to carry you to freedom. Follow the drinking gourd.'"

"I remember Miz Lizbet used to sing that."

"Natcherly," Callie said, motioning for Homer and Will to come into the warmth of the little house. "It's a secret code telling us how to cross the Ohio River. This way's freedom."

Chapter Thirty-Three
FLOATING FEATHER

The shrill whistle sliced the air again. I could hear Jeep's heart hammering next to mine. I raised my head off the ground to see what the whistle-blowing woman would do. Mike cussed under his breath, or maybe it was a prayer. On the other side, the dog was flipping his tail and licking Jeep's face like an ice-cream cone, and I heard Jeep whisper, "Whoa, boy, that tickles."

"Dog's a good judge of character," the woman said. "You can get up." Her voice seemed small for her square icebox build. Dusting off my jeans, I could finally look at her closely. She wore a huge turquoise-and-silver squash-blossom necklace and about a dozen rings, and she carried a twenty-pound bag of dog food over her shoulder like a baby, like it weighed nothing.

"Who are you kiddos?" she asked.

Jeep elbowed Mike, who elbowed me, who said the first thing that popped into my mind. "Who are *you?*" Good stall!

"I'm Faith Cloud, from next door. I feed Wolf while Mattie is gone."

"The dog's name is Wolf?" asked Mike.

"Look at him. He's no Tinkerbell," Jeep said. He was starting to regain his dignity after being face-down in the dust.

Now Wolf was on his hind legs, nosing the bag of dog food and Faith's underarms. "Wolf just loves my Ban Roll-On. Down, boy. Who did you say you were?"

"I'm Dana. I'm, uh, Mattie's niece."

"Oh, honey, she talks about you all the time. I hope you didn't come far, because Mattie's gone for a few days."

I put the back of my hand to my brow in a stage gesture. "Oh, I'm so disappointed. I wanted to surprise her on her birthday."

"Today's not her birthday. She's a Taurus, same as me."

"No, on *my* birthday. Did I say 'her birthday?'"

"This very day is your birthday? Well, how 'bout that! Listen, come on over to Faith's house, kiddos, and we'll put a candle in a Twinkie. It's the least I can do for Mattie's niece. Mattie's just the dearest neighbor old Faith Cloud's ever known, and I've lived awhile, you bet. How old do you think I am? Go ahead, guess."

"I dunno," Jeep said. "Fifty-seven?"

Faith grimaced as if she had a sudden gas pain. "Pushing fifty. Me and Mattie were born the very same day, and Mattie and me being next-door neighbors, can you beat that?"

The way she kept saying *Mattie* and not *Mattie and Raymond* gave me a brilliant hunch. "I haven't met my aunt's new husband. Is he a nice man?"

Faith's eyes clouded over. "She deserves better. Who are these handsome gents with you? Come, we'll all shake hands on the way over to Faith's house."

She led us into her sunny back porch, three walls of which were picture windows. It was her studio. Canvases stood stacked against the house wall, and the redbrick floor was covered with a crunchy tarp under the easel where Faith's current project dripped thick globs of paint.

"Don't touch that canvas, it's wet," she reminded us as she went to the kitchen for iced tea and Twinkies.

We all stared at the bold blotches of crimson, yellow, and fuchsia pink. The thick pockets of paint looked like coagulated body fluids.

"I don't get the concept," Jeep said. "The only thing I recognize is this white feather." It was a genuine feather, not paint, and it looked like it had just floated down and its vein had stuck onto the wet canvas. It fluttered gently in the breeze from the north window.

Faith came out with a loaded tray. "Do you like it?" she asked shyly.

Mike made a face, but Jeep covered for him. "The feather's really cool."

"Oh, it's more than cool." She handed each of us

a glass. The tea was milky, as though it had sat in the fridge for a week. "It's a Lenni Lenape legend."

"Who's Lenni Lenape?" asked Jeep.

"That's our name, my tribe. In our language it means *the real people*." Faith's laughter was like the tinkling of glass bells. "You probably think you're the real people," she said, pointing to Jeep. "What do you call yourselves these days? Afro Americans? American Africans? Ho! People try to call us Native Americans, but you can ask any one of us, and we'll tell you. We're Indians, and proud of it!"

Chapter Thirty-Four
March 1857
AN OLD GOOFER

Wonderful heat radiated off the walls of the fishermen's hut. Suddenly James felt a rumbling beneath his feet when the floor started rising! He jumped aside. Sabetha's eyes peered out of a two-inch slot.

"Mama, that you?" Callie threw the trapdoor open and pulled her mother up into the room. Miz Pru followed, with Solomon behind her.

James was never so glad to see anybody! He watched Solomon get taller with each step as he gently pushed Miz Pru up through the trapdoor. And didn't Miz Pru come up talking, as usual!

"Smell better up here. All of you's here?" she asked. By now she'd shed all her turkey feathers and hemp stalks and was no bigger than Callie. "How am I gonna know if I don't hear your voices, tell me that?"

"I be here, Mama Pru." Homer hugged his mother and shyly placed the red ball in her hand. She dropped that ball like it was a steaming potato. Maybe she knew it had been in the dogs' mouths, and Homer's, and every possible unsavory place between here and there.

Miz Pru petted Homer's thick square of woolly hair and asked, "How 'bout that stubborn white boy?"

"I'm here," Will assured her.

"And the one talks so pretty?"

"Thee can count on me, Miz Pru."

"Well, then." A smile spread across her face, which was the color of pecans but as wrinkled as a walnut shell. James noticed that her hands were wrinkled, too, and stained from sorting hemp plants by feel alone.

Callie had told James, "Miz Pru looks like she's a hundred years old, but she's no more than fifty-five or sixty. Conjurers don't age smooth like regular folks. She used to pick cotton down in Alabama till the master sold her North along with her husband. Her life was a little easier at Bullocks', but Miz Pru, she worked just like the rest of the field hands, from can see to can't see."

"What's that?" James had asked.

"For a smart Northern white boy, you sure don't know much. That means from sunrise to sunset."

Now Callie was clunking a wooden spoon against a black cast-iron kettle that hung over the hearth. "You smell something good, Mama Pru?"

The old woman sniffed the air, and Solomon said, "Lizbet, she told me all about these fishermen who leave a shack open for any of us to come home, leave something simmering over the embers for our empty bellies."

"Wouldn't none of you have found it, though, if I hadn't *seen* it in my back mind. Didn't I tell you, James Weaver?" Callie swirled the wooden spoon around in the kettle and lifted a hot, grayish spoonful to her lips. "Potato soup," she announced with such abiding pleasure that they all raced to the hearth to have a taste.

James longed to drop a dipper into that kettle and pull himself up a feast, but he saw the eager eyes of the others, heard Miz Pru smacking her lips, and he drew back to wait his turn. In his *back mind* he tasted sweet bits of onion, a mooshy chunk of potato big enough to fill his whole mouth. Salt stung his lips from this marvelous soup, so hot that it burned his throat as it slid down toward his growling belly. He watched Callie slip a spoonful into Miz Pru's mouth, careful to catch every drop in her hand below the old woman's chin.

Miz Pru said, "Needs pepper. Fishermen can't cook worth nothing." She reached out and squeezed James's arm. "I've felt snakes thicker than you. Talking pretty ain't gonna get you no meat on your bones. Take you some of this potato soup."

Gladly!

While Sabetha ladled them up mugs of soup, Miz Pru held court. "Me, I like a man with meat on his bones. My Sully, now there was a fleshy man."

Solomon sat on the floor at Miz Pru's knees, warming his hands on the mug of soup Sabetha had just given him. "Miz Lizbet used to talk some about her daddy, Sully."

"Old Sully, he worked at the hemp factory over in town," Miz Pru continued. "Came home every Saturday night, and Law, didn't we have a time!"

"Where Daddy be now?" Homer asked, from the floor on the other side of Miz Pru.

She clipped the side of his head. "How many times I gotta tell you, baby, your daddy with Jesus." Turning back to the rest of them, she added, "The Monday Fever done it, sucking in all that hemp dust till he was breathing through wet sponges in his chest."

Sabetha said, "You don't have to talk about it if it makes you sad, Miz Pru."

"Only thing makes me sad is Sully never held to my conjuring. Called me an old goofer. Said, 'Prudence Biggers, you be attending to our daughter, Lizbet, not half the folks between here and Aferka. You got magic, girl? Use it on that poor, simple-minded boy of ours, or Homer ain't gonna live long enough to get free with all the smarts the Lord done give him.'"

"Yes, suh, the Lord done give me smarts!"

Miz Pru grabbed his chin and squeezed his cheeks together until his lips puckered. "Well, jest look. Me and Homer outlived Sully Biggers by years." Shoving Homer's face aside, she reached out for Solomon's hand, which she worked like she was wringing out wash. "If only my Lizbet could have lived to see us sitting here drinking soup like the rich white folks. Solomon, reckon she's home free?"

"Yes, ma'am," Solomon said quietly. "Miz Lizbet Charles is about the freest person I ever knew."

Their bellies full, Miz Pru dozing in the only chair, they sat on the floor talking about what to do next, and then they heard the door of the shack inch open on creaky hinges. Solomon scrambled to his feet and pulled Miz Pru's chair into a shadowy corner, and the others scurried behind Solomon and James, as if they could hide in this one little room.

Will leaned against the wall and lifted his crutch for a weapon as a man poked his face in. An animal-skin hat was pulled to his pitcher ears. "Name's Clooney. You folks is safe," he said. His voice was scratchy, as if he'd been shouting into the wind all day.

"Safe from *what*?" Will asked. "Could be a trickster."

Callie yanked the raised crutch out of Will's hand. "It's one of the fishermen. Gray beard, white hair, beaver hat, just the way I saw him in my back mind."

"You sure?" James whispered.

"Ask him does he have a finger missing."

The fisherman stepped into the room holding up his left fist and let his fingers spring open. Four fingers. Clooney said, "No time to waste, folks. Ferry's waiting."

"Indiana," said Callie dreamily as they all scrambled off the ferry on the north bank of the Ohio River. "I've been hearing about this place all my life." She dug her toes into the rich soil. "I believe I'll just take root right here and grow like that sycamore."

Clooney tamped the earth with his scuffed-up brogans and said, "You've got a ways to go yet, folks. Fact is, there's peril every road you walk— slave catchers for hire to send you back South, even runaways themselves who've gotten free and turned against their own kind for cold money."

Sabetha said, "I just don't believe they'd *do* that."

Miz Pru huffed, "What's all this I been hearing about being home free once you cross the river?"

The fisherman nodded soberly. "You heard right, ma'am, more or less." He gazed back across the river and stroked his dangly sideburns, as if searching for words that wouldn't scare them too badly. "All I'm saying is, just watch who you trust." And he gave Solomon the location of a farmhouse within a night's walk. "You'll be in safe harbor there. Folks there can send you on to the next place, and that place knows the next one and so on. It's the only way this Underground Railroad works worth spit."

James said, "Thee's been very kind, Mr. Clooney."

"What's that you called me? You never heard my name. All you know about me and my buddy is, we catch fish for the steamboats, catch 'em and sell 'em. What else we do and who we are, why, it's nobody's business, you get me?" He doffed his beaver cap at the ladies and shook hands with all the gentlemen.

Homer grinned and pumped Clooney's hand as if he were drawing water from a well, and the fisherman said to him, "You take care of these ladies, hear? See they get safe to their destination."

"Yes, suh!"

Chapter Thirty-Five
GIFT OF FEATHERS

The sunlight shone brilliant and clear on Faith Cloud's porch. The only thing that wasn't clear was her iced tea, and I wondered what it had been used for in its previous life. Mike actually took a sip of that stuff, but then Mike can chew up jalapeño peppers like some people chew popcorn.

He asked Faith about the Lenni Lenape legend.

Faith tilted her head and said coyly, "Oh, I'll tell it, but first let's refresh ourselves with my secret-recipe tea."

It flitted through my mind that Faith might be a crazy woman and we'd all be poisoned by her strange brew, but she took great swallows of it, and besides, Wolf seemed to trust her. Still, I set my glass behind a plant.

Faith looked out the window as though she were reading the legend in the trees and wind. "We believe a great guardian spirit hovers in the sky and looks after us."

"Yeah, it's called God," Mike said, as though he'd heard it all.

"Maybe," Faith conceded. "But with Indian

peoples, God takes lots of different forms. For the Lenni Lenape, he's an eagle with wings spread real wide to shelter us. When we do things he doesn't like, he makes the rain flood our rivers until they're overflowing their banks. My people say that the thunder is his angry roar, and the lightning is the flashing of his angry eyes. You don't want to be in his path when he's mad, no way!"

I glanced over at Mike. He was sitting at the edge of the rattan chair, intrigued and pouring his tea into a yucca plant beside him.

"But when we do things that please him, he's real generous, like a father. He makes the corn grow tall, and the buffalo herds dense and plentiful enough for whatever we need." Faith finished her tea and didn't keel over, so I sipped mine, too. It tasted like the codeine cough medicine I forced down last winter.

"Of course, that's our job—to please the Great Eagle Spirit, and sometimes we do, and sometimes we don't. We're only human, you know. But sometimes we go way past his expectations, and times like that he'll let a feather float down from way up there to let us know he's proud that we've been put down here to share this sweet, sweet, green earth."

"That's the feather in the painting?" Mike asked.

"Oh, yes, he's *real* pleased with my work." Her weathered face broke into a grin, and she cradled her hands between her knees. "But there's more. When you've got the gift of one of these feathers, when you hold it to your face, to your body, nothing can harm you. My language doesn't translate just right into English, but you could say that when this happens, you're *in*. *In*vulnerable, *in*vincible, and *in*visible."

"Wow! How come we can still see you?" Jeep asked.

"I'm letting you, is why."

Mike said, "I've lived in Kansas all my life. I've heard of the Cherokee and the Pawnee and the Shawnee and the Kiowa and the Comanche, but I've never heard of the Lenni Lenape."

"Of course not," Faith said. "Oh, my, this isn't right." She turned her head this way and that to study the canvas. She flattened a blob of red paint with the palm of her hand. A fortune-teller would be able to read the lines of Faith's skin in the paint. "There, that's better. No, you wouldn't recognize the name Lenni Lenape. It's our own name. The white man calls us Delaware."

Delaware! More pieces were coming together.

"You know, kiddos, the Delawares own the land you're sitting on. Or should, if the government hadn't screwed it all up. My too-many-greats-to-count-grandfather, he had the papers to prove it. Wrote all about it in a book."

Jeep pinched my arm, and I said, "Was his name Straightfeather?" Faith Cloud's eyes got wide as I said, "I've seen the book."

172

"Oh, honey, you couldn't have. There were only ten copies printed, and the only one left on the whole blamed planet was my own, which got stolen this past winter, along with my *tee*-vee and VCR. Those thieves, I hope they're enjoying my *tee*-vee, or got good money for it. But I sure do grieve for that book."

Chapter Thirty-Six
March 1857
THE DEVILS IN THE CAVE

They hid in a barn with either Solomon or Will standing guard all through the day. It stung James that he hardly ever got guard duty, not that he'd be any kind of hero if someone stumbled onto their camp in broad daylight. Nevertheless he stayed awake most of the day just in case Solomon or Will dozed off and some farmer came tearing across the field with a pitchfork meant for the hayloft where Callie and Sabetha slept.

It was seventeen days since James had left home; it seemed like a year.

Miz Pru had a plug of tobacco in her cheek, and she was chawing away at it. "Good for wasp stings," she told James when he saw her spit the black sinews of tobacco on the sawdust floor.

Sabetha said, "Miz Pru, that's just about the ugliest thing I've seen."

Miz Pru just scowled and retorted, "If I ain't eatin', at least I kin be chewin'."

Now, as the sun fell behind the barn, they bustled around preparing for another dark night of stealing away under a canopy of stars.

Even if he were a rotten watch guard, at least James could keep everyone's spirits up, so he fairly chirped: "By the day after tomorrow we'll be at the place the farmer sent us, sleeping in a proper room."

Miz Pru grumbled, "I done slept next to a horse on the scratchiest of horse blankets this day. Y'all know what a horse smell like? And chickens walking acrost me all night? I sure could use me a bed tomorra."

James's heart sank. "I'm sorry, Miz Pru, but tomorrow Solomon says we'll be sleeping in a cave near New Harmony, Indiana."

"Hunh-uh, hunh-uh, no, suh," Homer cried. "No cave, ain't gonna sleep in no cave." Homer began bashing his head against the wall until half the barn rattled and the scrawny horse got spooked.

Sabetha threw her arms around Homer. "Hold still. You'll loosen those nails, and the walls are gonna fall down around us." She clutched him and calmed him and pulled him down to the ground beside her. He sat on his knees and rocked back and forth. "Hunh-uh," he kept saying, "no cave, nosuh-nosuhnosuh."

Sabetha stroked his huge hand and explained about his fear. She had a way of talking to you without ever looking at you, so some of her words floated away toward the horse, but James caught the gist of it.

175

"When Homer was nine, maybe ten, he was sold away from Miz Pru. He was a big boy. He could all but lift a horse, so master got a good price for him. But seller and buyer, neither one knew he was half gone in the head."

Miz Pru took up the story. "Homer's job was to fetch water for the field hands. They was working tobacco. That new master, he rigged up a pole with buckets on each end and sent Homer down into hell."

"Ma'am?" James asked, and Sabetha explained, "Homer went twenty, thirty feet down into this cave, where the water pooled."

"Hunh-uh, hunh-uh, no cave." Homer fidgeted like he was kneeling on an anthill.

"Homer's daddy—"

"My Sully," Miz Pru interrupted, "he was *some* storyteller. Back when Homer was still wetting his britches, Sully used to tell about the devils and mon-ster-beasts that lived in the caves, just a-waiting for poor little colored boys. Law, they was a lot of them, and they all had horns and eyes that burned in the dark, and teeth like needles and skin they slimed right outta."

Homer twitched and moaned, and his mother's bones cracked as she knelt behind him on the ground to rub his neck. His head lolled on his shoulders.

"You tell the rest, Sabetha."

"Homer had to go down into that cave, so scared

he was about frozen like a pillar of salt. On a good, sunny day, the light would shine from behind, and he'd see his way, mostly. But on a cloudy day like this one, he'd go down, down, down in that damp, skittery darkness. Imagine it."

The skin on James's back crawled, and he drew himself into a tighter package.

"My poor boy Homer, he never could tell me just what he saw down there, 'least not in words, not after seven years when master gave up on him and sent him home to me. Didn't even reconize my own boy grown into a man."

After a long, hushed time, James said, "I'll speak to Solomon, Homer. I expect he'll have thee stand guard all night while the rest of us sleep in the cave, if that's to thy liking."

Homer sat up straight and still, as if he'd heard a distant bell. "I can do that," he said. "I ain't afraid of nothin' 'cept that cave."

On the fifth day out they reached the home of the Reverend Thomas Snowbird. Mrs. Snowbird had a girlish voice and two chattery daughters who flanked her, all of them in bell-shaped dresses that swayed as they walked. A shelf along the south wall was loaded with rough-hewn pottery and daguerreotypes of stern ancestors, and the big family Bible. Mrs. Snowbird pressed a button behind the Bible, and suddenly the wall swung back to reveal a secret room.

"There's another just like it beyond that wall," she said, nodding to each of her daughters, "isn't that right, girls?"

James was thrilled by what he saw: four cots with fluffy pillows and blankets, chamber pots, a blue-and-white ceramic washbasin and pitcher, and a small crate shelf stacked with books.

Will said, "Why, it's a regular pitcher and catcher place!"

"I beg your pardon?" Mrs. Snowbird said.

"A pitcher to wash with, and a chamber pot to catch—well, I reckon you know what."

Mrs. Snowbird's hands fluttered around her red face. "I declare."

And what was this beautiful thing that James spotted over in the corner? A huge galvanized tub. A bath!

While the ladies settled in the back room and the men in the first room, Mrs. Snowbird and her daughters boiled kettles of water, which the Reverend Mr. Snowbird carried and poured into the tubs. James heard giggles beyond the wall as Callie sloshed around in her tub. As for the men, they drew straws for the first bath, and Will won. Eagerly he ripped off his filthy clothes and dropped them into a miserable heap. Something with at least six legs crawled out from under the heap.

James caught sight of Will's bare stump for the first time. The leg was ghost white and stopped about halfway to the knee. It had healed in jagged lumps of florid flesh.

All at once Will grew self-conscious and flung himself over the side of the tub, making a whale's splash.

"Sorry," James murmured.

"No need." Will soaped himself with a grim look on his face until his whole chest was covered with lather and clouds of lather floated on the gray wash water.

After Will's and James's baths, the tub was refilled for Solomon and Homer. Solomon was used to hot baths from living with Dr. Olney's family, but this bath was Homer's first soaker. Modestly he kept his shirt tied around his middle until he'd lowered himself into the water still foamy from Solomon's bath. Once he hit bottom, the shirt came flying out of the tub. Homer slid under until his knees were up against the wall of the tub and water bobbled around his chin.

"Ahhh," he said, "ahhh," as Solomon poured another kettle of hot water into the tub before the bath got too cold to be pure heaven. "Ahhhhh . . ."

Chapter Thirty-Seven
A POLITICALLY CORRECT INDIAN

On the way back to Lawrence, Howie sang along with some of the worst classic country-western music still permitted on the airwaves—Willie Nelson and Tammy Wynette and Hank Williams. He had a nasal twang to beat all of them. The rest of us speculated on the possibilities that Faith Cloud had opened up.

Mike said, "Let's say Faith was this Straightfeather guy's great-great-great-granddaughter."

"Had to be back six generations," Jeep said. "Do the math."

"Right, so let's say Straightfeather was about forty-eight when Miz Lizbet died in 1857."

"That would put him taking his first breath in 1809."

It was too fast for me. I was still counting back six generations on my fingers. I do people, not numbers; numbers make me break out in a cold sweat. I said, "And let's say dear old neighbor Mattie steals Faith Cloud's prized family possession, that book that just happens to be in Mattie's suitcase at my house."

"Doesn't compute," Jeep said. "What about the TV and VCR?"

Mike was turned around, hanging over the front seat like a drunken sailor. "They're for cover so she wouldn't notice the book gone too soon. Say more, Dana."

"Mattie reads in the book about a promise the government made to the Delaware tribe but never kept. It's all spelled out in a document or something. Mattie wants to find that sucker for—what for, guys?"

"Maybe she's a Delaware," Jeep mused.

"I doubt it. Faith would have said so. Yeow!" Mike's head hit the roof of the car as Howie flew over a bump.

Then Howie finally said something worth listening to besides his thumping country-western beat on the dashboard. "Can't you find some old Indian lying around Lawrence?"

It wasn't a bad idea, but you can't let Howie have too much credit. "Just how do you find such a guy, Howie?"

Mike said, "Easy. You put an ad in the paper. 'Wanted: Indian. Must be over 120 years old.'"

I laughed. "Great, but what if a Cherokee or Kiowa turns up? We've got to be more specific. Besides, some people are offended by the term *Indian*."

"Yeah, like the term *Negro* insults black people

now," Jeep said, "even though it's cooler than any-thing else they called us back in Miz Lizbet's day."

"Hmmn, this is tough," Mike said. "Okay, how's this: 'Wanted: old Delaware—'"

"Can't say 'old.' Say 'senior citizen.'"

"'Wanted: Senior-citizen Delaware man—'"

"That's sexist. Say 'person.'"

"'Wanted: Senior-citizen Delaware person of Native-American ancestry.'"

"'Ancestry' suggests racism. Say 'persuasion.'"

"I give up." Mike turned around and propped his heels on the dashboard.

My parents were both out when we got back to Firebird House. This was my big chance! I raced upstairs to the Berks' room to have a good look at Faith Cloud's stolen book.

The room was still a mess of rumpled sheets and towels and candy wrappers, but all of the Berks' things were gone. Dad later told me that the police had packed everything up and had taken it all as evidence.

Now, more than ever, I needed an actual Indian. I told my dad what I knew he'd love to hear, that I'd suddenly gotten deeply interested in Plains Indian history, and I asked if anyone in his department at the university studied local tribes, like, oh, I don't know, maybe . . . the Delaware?

Even better. He had a graduate student who was

doing a combined dissertation in history and anthropology on Native American folk customs, and she was interviewing several people to get their stories. Her name was Tracy. When I phoned her, she had great news:

"I've got just the man for you, Dana. His name is Bo Prairie Fire. He's an old Delaware Indian, and he's very willing to talk. Talks nonstop, in fact."

"Great!"

"There's a catch," the girl said playfully. "Mr. Bo Prairie Fire just doesn't make a whole lot of sense."

Chapter Thirty-Eight
March 1857
RATS AND AMBROSIA

James thought little of the insistent rap on the door until one of the Snowbird girls said, "Hush!" and slid the secret panel shut. Now the little room felt like a cage and James an animal not fit to roam free. He listened closely.

"Good day, Reverend Snowbird. I regret the intrusion, Mrs. Snowbird, this being the Sabbath Day, but I've got reason to believe you're, shall we say, exceeding the capacity of your household."

James motioned for the men to come listen at the wall, and Callie tiptoed over as well. Ears pressed to the movable wall, they heard an astonishing conversation that said nothing and everything at the same time.

First Mrs. Snowbird said, "Have a seat, Mayor Blanchard. Lettie, bring the mayor a piece of your blueberry cobbler."

"I don't want to put you out, Mrs. Snowbird."

"Nonsense. Lettie Lou puts up the finest blueberries. I tell you, a treat is about to delight your tongue."

The girls scurried across the kitchen after the cobbler, a plate, a fork, maybe a cup of tea, then the mayor's voice came through clearly. "I'm no dough-face, mind you, no advocate, I say no *advocate,* of slavery. I'd never let that peculiar institution flourish in my town or anywhere else in the state of Indiana if I had a say."

"I'm sure you wouldn't, Mayor Blanchard."

The mayor cleared his throat. "But there are laws, Pastor Snowbird, and the one I can quote you chapter and verse—if you'll forgive my using church terminology in vain—has to do with how it's against the law to shelter runaway Negroes who are legally, I say *legally,* the property of some of our brethren dwelling in the South."

Reverend Snowbird said, "There's law and there's *law.*"

A plate clattered down on the table, followed by the bustling of skirts and crinolines as the Snowbird girls apparently settled into chairs.

"Indeed. Yet, I remind you, Pastor, there are fine gentlemen not unlike yourself with bounties on their heads. Perhaps you've heard about the Reverend Mr. John Rankin over in Ohio?"

"No, sir, I have not."

"Ah," the mayor said, his mouth full of cobbler. The next few words were garbled. ". . . slave owners are offering a reward of two thousand five hundred dollars for the Reverend Rankin's head. Not his head, per se, although his assassination has been mentioned in some circles."

Mrs. Snowbird said, "Oh mercy on men who would do such a dastardly thing."

"Quite right." Mayor Blanchard apparently took a sip of tea, for James heard the cup clang in the saucer. "Let me be straightforward. I come, shall we say, as an ambassador representing your parishioners. They believe, I say they *truly* believe, that this house they provide for you and yours, free of any cost whatsoever, is modest, to their eternal shame. One would say it's just about big enough for a man and his wife and two or three robust children. Any more occupants than that, why, your church family begins to wonder if they're providing for you, shall we say, inadequately. Do I make myself clear?"

"I understand you perfectly, Mayor Blanchard," the pastor said. "Of course, you're welcome to lift that tablecloth or look under the beds or in my daughters' trousseau trunks just in case we might be hiding Negroes. I recommend you tap each wall, sir, to be sure no one's lurking behind them."

James heard Callie suck in her breath as the mayor said, "Why, Reverend Snowbird, I'd never doubt the word of a man of God. I only speak for the good people of this town and the members of Countryside Christian Church, to whom you are, shall we say, beholden."

"Thank you for your concern," the pastor said.

Just then Homer dropped his red rubber ball.

Thud! It scuttled under a bed. James held his breath until he heard Lettie Lou yell, "Rats! Papa, you promised you'd set a trap."

"Yes, Papa," echoed her sister. The rockers thumped as she leaped from her chair. "Lettie and I will just die if we have to come face-to-face with a ring-tailed rat. Die, Papa, we'll just swoon and die right here on the floor." She stamped her foot a few solid times while Homer slid under the bed to recapture his prized ball.

The mayor said, "It might not be a rat at all, little ladies. We had a raccoon in our attic just this past winter that gave Mrs. Blanchard apoplexy. Just the same," the mayor said, his voice turning hard once again, "I believe I'd set a trap." Then there was the scraping of chairs and the mayor speaking again. "Well, Mrs. Blanchard is waiting for me to escort her over to Sutton's mill. I shall take leave of you fine people. Lettie Lou, your cobbler was ambrosia, pure *ambrosia,* I must say."

After the door closed, there came a light *tappity-tap* on the sliding wall: all clear. Only then did James breathe in and out, steady and regular.

Chapter Thirty-Nine
BO PRAIRIE FIRE

Mr. Bo Prairie Fire lived in a homeless shelter. He could have been ninety, or maybe only sixty, and he was about one notch short of totally crazy. They say being homeless does that to a person.

On Tuesday the grad student, Tracy, and I went to visit Mr. Prairie Fire on the second-floor screened porch of the shelter. A dozen people stood around us, blowing cigarette smoke out through the screens. They wore every odd piece of clothing you can imagine: paint-crusted overalls, ski masks that left only their noses and mouths exposed, skin-tight Lycra. One lady had four skinny fur bodies draped over her shoulders with black stub noses, and sad eyes that had seen it all. She said they were her fox martens, a wedding present from her husband about sixty years before. Besides that, nobody had much to say except Mr. Prairie Fire, who couldn't be stopped. I scribbled notes while he spoke like a tape at dub speed.

"Land, we had land, land, land. They take it. White man. We come from Pennsylvania. They push us west, west to this spot, not even called Kansas Territory yet. Here we make a home, up by the river, the Kansas River, where it meets the Missouri River, our land. You know the place?"

"I've been there, Mr. Prairie Fire. In fact—"

"Narrow strip of land by the mouth of the two rivers. Belongs to my people, a thousand people. People of the corn. Fall Leaf; ever hear of him? A chief. Early this year he finds gold in the western part of the territory. Some call it Colorado. But our land's in the east. Northeast corner, up near Leavenworth. Land, land, two hundred thousand acres." His eyes raced wildly, as if a movie were flickering past them. "My grandfathers are buried there. Six, seven, eight generations, nine, ten.

"Tepees, we live in tepees. How do we keep them from blowing over? Kansas wind blows all the time, girlie, night and day." Mr. Prairie Fire paused to take a puff of his cigarette, which he inhaled deeply. His gray hair hung almost to his waist but was thin on top, where brown age spots dotted his head.

"We cross lodgepoles, we bind them with rawhide. Know what rawhide is? We drop a strip of it from the center and anchor it on a peg in the ground. Dry ground. Not enough rain. Some years the corn doesn't grow. Heavy rocks hold the edges of the tepees, keep them from blowing over in the wind. White man moves us. We have to move fast, move fast. We pick up the tepees and take them with us. You can see the circle of stones left over. Go and see."

"Wasn't this a long time ago, Mr. Prairie Fire?" I asked.

"Long time ago. Eighteen and thirty, eighteen and forty. Yesterday. Go and see." He stubbed his cigarette out on the cement floor and immediately lit another one. "I'm a turkey." He paused to let that fact sink in, but I didn't follow. He pulled his feet up on the couch with amazing grace and propped his chin on his knees. "We have three clans. Wolf. Turtle. Turkey. I'm Turkey Clan. Twelve," he said, looking at me sternly.

"Twelve, sir?"

"Yes, yes! It takes twelve shouts to reach the ear of the Great Spirit up in the twelfth heaven." He demonstrated the shouts, which sent the lightbulb in the ceiling swinging. I expected the bulb to shatter. I resisted covering my ears.

"South wind, north wind, they play dice."

Plainly the man was nuts.

"Captain John Ketchum, chief of the Lenni Lenape, my people, the real people. He died yesterday, you know."

"Yesterday?" I asked. Funny, I hadn't seen anything about it in the paper even though I was scrounging for every piece of information I could ferret out on the Delaware people.

Gently, Tracy probed him. "Mr. Prairie Fire, what year is it now?"

"The year Chief Ketchum dies. Yesterday. Eighteen and fifty-seven."

Chapter Forty
March 1857
SHPRINTZE'S CALICO

Heading north and west across Illinois, they stumbled through fifteen to twenty miles each night. Callie and Will took the miles like frisky pups. James felt himself growing heartier with each night's traveling. Thick wads of muscle balled in his calves, and his back was now strong enough to bear his pack and Miz Pru's, both. Solomon and Sabetha plodded along, trailing the younger folks, and most of the way Homer carried Miz Pru on his back.

"If I wasn't blind as an ear of corn, I could do this on my own," the old woman groused. Every so often she'd slide down his back and bark, "Can't any of you see in the dark any better than I can, so I might as well walk," and she'd thrust an end of her leash rope into Homer's hand.

One morning just before dawn, a wagon slowed to pick them up. The driver was an immigrant peddler with a bushy beard, strange fringes hanging below his shirt, and an accent James could barely decipher.

"My wife, Shprintze, calls me Shmuel," he said

in his singsongy style. "Sam is good enough." He lifted Miz Pru onto the seat beside him and tucked a red plaid blanket around her legs. "You've been on the road a long time?" He tried not to wrinkle his nose, but James could just imagine how ripe they all must smell.

He explained, "We've been sleeping in haylofts and on horse blankets and in caves and out in the pouring rain."

"We had baths," Will reminded him.

Shmuel sniffed the air. "When, last Christmas?" He said it like "Krrrissmuhss."

"Three days ago," Will responded indignantly. "But we didn't have any clean clothes to change into."

"I'm afraid we must smell like skunks to thee."

The peddler chuckled. "Shprintze has a milch cow that stinks sweeter." He signaled for all of them to climb into the back of his wagon and to find niches around his barrels and crates of merchandise.

Miz Pru sat with her back prim and straight, careful not to spill over onto Shmuel's side of the bench. It occurred to James that she'd probably never sat so close to a white man before.

Shmuel sang,

> *"I've got needles, I've got thread,*
> *Pots and pans, apples and bread.*

192

I've got scissors, saucers, and snuff,
Tins of marmalade, coffee enough.
I've got buttons, snappers, and hooks,
A bucket of pickles, a barrel of books.
I've got roads to travel, rain and snow,
And yards of Shprintze's calico."

Sabetha looked longingly at the bolts of fabric, and the thought of orange marmalade smeared on about six of Ma's biscuits made James's head swirl. He leaned into Shmuel's back and replied, "I'm sorry, sir, but we have little money and what we have left we must save for the steamboat tickets in St. Louis."

Shmuel nodded. "I am also running, friends."

"You, suh?" asked Miz Pru, barely turning her head.

"Of course, missus. Why else would I leave my little village in the Carpathians? Leave my parents, my grandparents, of blessed memory, and flee with my wife and children across the ocean? To see the world? Hah! We ran for our lives." Shmuel gently urged the old piebald nag onward, and she glanced back at him for sympathy.

Homer jumped out of the wagon. "I kin walk. That beast ain't able to tote this bigga load."

Solomon and Sabetha scrambled to the ground as well, and the horse seemed very relieved.

They all spent the day outside of Shmuel's

hut near Centralia, Illinois. Shprintze gave them mounds of her sweet noodle pudding, which they washed down with milk still warm from her fragrant cow. Later they slept while Shprintze and her daughter sewed swaths of calico into colorful shifts for Callie and Miz Pru and Sabetha.

At dusk they left with a basket of bread and carrots and potatoes and the red plaid blanket from the wagon.

"Go in good health," Shmuel called as they began their trek toward Belleville.

That night, though, things turned sour. Miz Pru was having fits because she'd run out of chewing tobacco. She agitated Homer so much that he set her down in a meadow and walked away. They'd covered a mile before anyone noticed, and Solomon had to double back to fetch the woman.

Callie and James felt achy and weak with ague, and Miz Pru set a few twigs afire to boil the bark of a cottonwood tree. She applied the brew to their aching limbs with her usual rough strokes that felt like urging slaps on a horse's rump. James didn't mention his scratchy throat; no telling *what* nasty tea she'd make him swallow, or what kind of a poultice she'd wrap around his neck.

Sabetha was irritable and snapped at Solomon half the night. She stepped into a declivity, turned her ankle, and blamed Solomon the other half of the night. James could see the tension in Solomon's shoulders, hunched with his and Sabetha's heavy packs. Finally Solomon said, "We've been traveling eleven nights now, twenty-six for Mr. Will and Mr. James and me. We all need a night of rest." He dropped the two packs to the ground beside a creek and was asleep before anyone could argue.

The unexpected holiday turned their moods around. Miz Pru conjured up several catfish in the swollen creek and scattered flannel mullein seeds over them to stun them so James and Will could catch them by hand. "Won't hurt human folks none," she assured them as the stupefied fish floated languidly close to the surface.

Will lit a roaring fire—a chancy gamble, but with Solomon asleep, no one protested. They huddled around the fire that was turning the tough, bony catfish into a feast. Sabetha set half a potato and a mess of carrot peels on the embers for each of them as well.

Homer said, "Honey Sabetha, y'all lookin' right pretty in the firelight."

"I'm a mess!" She slid her hands together like she was rolling dough. "How come nobody told me how cold it is up here in the North?"

Miz Pru stuck her bare feet toward the fire. "She's a Southern girl, that one. Born in Alabama."

Sabetha scooped the potatoes and carrot peelings onto a tin plate with a little juice dripped from the fish, and she set the plate over the fire. "You think Bullocks' is a plantation? Hunh-uh, it's a measly no-account little old hemp farm. I grew up on a real plantation, cotton, three hundred field hands if there was one."

Callie said, "Tell them, Mama."

"Ooh, yes, a big plantation. My mama picked cotton side by side with the men, but when I came along in her, she got puny and sickly, could barely keep up. Here I came out, way too early, and my mama was no good in the field anymore."

"No good, no, suh." Homer provided the chorus.

"So master, he used her where she could work hard for him," Sabetha said, her voice sharp as tacks. "She had two more babies, both died." She sat back on her haunches while the fish sizzled and the peelings curled in the hot juices. "Sold Mama and me North to Bullocks. Threw us in, no charge, with two strapping men the size of Homer."

James asked, "How old was thee then?"

"Ten, twelve. Little time passed, and Mama had another baby, but that one killed her, and Bullocks, they just lost track of me with no mama and all. Miz Pru just took me in like her own. Her girl, Lizbet, she'd already been sold away soon as she got to looking pert."

"Sold away cold," Miz Pru murmured. She poked at the fish with a stick; the flesh seemed yielding, ready to eat.

Sabetha lifted the hot plate out of the fire with

the hem of her new dress. "And that's why Homer and Miz Pru and Callie and me, we're a family."

Homer pulled his seared potato out of the fire. "Honey Sabetha, you my sister and my sweetheart, both."

Sabetha gave Homer a withering look, unmistakable in the glow of the fire. "I ain't nobody's sweetheart. Now that I'm out of Bullocks' house, I'm my own woman, and don't you forget it for an eye blink, hear?"

Chapter Forty-One
LULU

The screened porch of the shelter was flooded with sunlight, but Mr. Prairie Fire still shivered. A wiry woman in a Hawaiian muumuu came cradling a blue plastic pan filled with water. "Don't mind me," she chirped. The dry, bloated wood screeched as she raised the screen and tossed the whole pan of water out the window. We heard it go *splat* three floors below. She turned around, flashed us a toothless grin, and said, "Somebody's gotta water the petunias, right, Bo?"

Mr. Prairie Fire brightened at her words. "That's my Lulu. Ain't she a dish? Y'oughta taste her fry bread, my Lulu's fry bread."

The woman came over and patted Mr. Prairie Fire's head. "Yeah, babe, I'm your Lulu, all right. I'm whipping up a batch of fry bread out in the tepee, babe. Oil's sizzling right now." Her words comforted Mr. Prairie Fire, but her eyes told us a different story.

When he was distracted by a fit of coughing, she said, "I don't mind that he thinks I'm his sweetheart Lulu. Hell's bells, some days I believe I am." She chuckled and left us with Mr. Prairie Fire. He'd dozed off, exhausted by his coughing, but he woke suddenly with his eyes blazing. "Yep," he said, "eighteen and fifty-seven, that's the year."

Tracy glanced at me, and I seized the opening. "Mr. Prairie Fire, did something special happen to your people this year, 1857?"

"Yes, yes! Indian agent came to our chiefs. Made promises to return land. Pay us back for trees and horses stolen, corn crops ruined. Made a treaty. Ghosts, ghosts."

Excitement pounding in my chest, I asked, "What happened to that treaty, sir?"

"Lies, all of it lies. No money came. White man comes back. Buys the land cheap. Steals it. We move, we pack up, fold the tepees. You can see the circles of rocks. Go and see. We move south to Indian Territory. Some call it Oklahoma."

"What year is it now, Mr. Prairie Fire," Tracy asked.

He looked at her as if she were missing some significant marbles. "I don't know what year it is in your life, girlie, but for the rest of us, it's eighteen and sixty-six. We're in Indian Territory. Land's gone, land by the Kansas and Missouri Rivers. We live with the Cherokee Nation. They don't want us. Don't even talk the same language."

While he stopped to puff on his cigarette, I jumped in with another question. "Mr. Prairie Fire, how do you know about this treaty if it was never signed or honored?"

"Straightfeather," he said, and my heart leaped. "He wrote a book. He was there, you know, when the treaty was signed by our chief, then, pfft, the treaty vanished like sage smoke. Gone."

"Mr. Prairie Fire," Tracy said gently, "Samuel Straightfeather has been dead about a hundred years."

"Is that so? Nobody told me." Suddenly Mr. Prairie Fire began to cry. Tracy handed him a tissue, and he dabbed delicately at his tears, which left fine snail tracings down his tanned-hide face. "Go away. You bring bad news."

Tracy nodded to me, and we gathered up our tape recorder and notebooks. "May we come back, Mr. Prairie Fire?"

"Not until the Doll Dance," he said, sounding like a stubborn child. "Do you have the doll?"

Tracy whispered to me, "The oldest in the clan must have the doll and perform the sacred Doll Dance."

"Well, do you?"

"No, sir, I'm sorry."

"Then don't come back." He turned his face to the wall as we left. I was embarrassed and confused and angry and glad to be out of that depressing house. But when we were getting into Tracy's car, someone whistled to us from the third-story porch, and it was a sound like a coyote. We looked up. Mr. Prairie Fire had opened the screen and was leaning out the window. "Girlie, come back tomorrow, I give you more."

Chapter Forty-Two
March 1857
DAWGS

In Belleville, Illinois, the Freemen Society hid the women and Solomon and Homer in the Negro section of the city. Two Freemen escorted Will and James to Hamilton Street, the edge of the Negro neighborhood, and gave them directions to a safe house for the day's rest.

It was at least an hour's walk through the richest section of the city, which held James in thrall. The streets were empty, since most people were still asleep. James studied each house they passed, observing the clean spaces between windows, the elevations of the doors, the brick and stone and stucco and wood, and all sorts of gewgaws and gargoyles that made each house distinctive. He sketched in his mind, fixing a window that seemed out of proportion, front steps too steep, chimneys that stuck up from the roofs as awkward as giraffes. And he filed away in his mind every detail that seemed beautifully fit to its purpose.

Will was yammering about something, which James ignored, until he felt a jolt to his arm. "James, look behind!"

Homer was following them. "Missuh James, Missuh Will, wait up."

James turned around. "Homer, it's not safe for thee to be in this neighborhood. Thee must go right back to Solomon and thy mother."

"Yes, suh, but I cain't stay in tha' house."

James sighed. Was it going to be the cave all over again? "Why not, Homer?"

"Ain't never see a color' person home so fancy as Miz Ophelia Simms's, no, suh. Ain't right."

Two elegant men stepped out of the hotel they were passing, and Will spun Homer around and stuffed him into a space under the building. Will and James scrambled up onto the fire escape, where they wouldn't be seen.

The men wore stovepipe hats and had gold watch fobs draped across their well-fed bellies. The one with white spats said to the other, older man, "Cyrus, I do believe that was a Negro person who darted under the hotel. What do you suppose the scalawag is doing under there?"

"Up to no good, you can be sure," the other man said.

Of course, neither wanted to get his fancy clothes dirty, so they grabbed a delivery boy walking by, and the one called Cyrus said, "Young man, you duck down under there and see if you spot a Negro. You can be sure he means trouble, sneaking around that way."

The boy crouched down and gazed under the

house. James held his breath, sure that Homer was doomed. Then a ferocious dog began to growl and yip under the house, and the boy jumped back and told the men, "I'm sorry, sirs, only thing under the hotel is a lot of dirt and a mad dog."

White Spats reached into his pocket and pulled out a silver coin, which he flicked with his thumb into the boy's hand. The two men walked on, having lost interest in Homer.

As soon as the street was clear, Will and James ran with Homer back to the Negro section. Safely across Hamilton Street, James said, "Thee was lucky, Homer, lucky that dog was under there with thee."

"Yes, suh, onee I be the dawg. I see these two blue eyes huntin' me out, and in my head I be hearin' my houns back at Bullocks'. Then this growl start up in my throat like Hannibal, and a coupla sharp barks comes out like Daisy. You shoulda see those two blue eyes jumpin' back in they head. Nex' thing I hear that boy say, 'Ain't nothing but a mad dog unner there.' Fool him, ole Homer did! Dawgs, they's mush in my hands."

That afternoon James and Will and Solomon met at Mrs. Ophelia Simms's brownstone to plan the next leg of the journey. Mrs. Simms was the richest Negro lady in Illinois. She owned two bakeries and a pool hall and a blacksmith shop. Fourteen people worked for her. Her front parlor was all done up in brocade and lace. James's ma would have turned her lip up at the showiness of it all. But Mrs. Simms and her family were good folks; they couldn't help being rich.

James asked, "Solomon, has thee got the papers?"

Solomon opened the flap on his leather pouch. Lamplight glinted off the stark-white inside. "Miz Simms's son, Otis, did up the papers like they're a whole family." Solomon took out the sheaf of parchment. "See? Mr. and Mrs. Homer Biggers, their daughter, Callie Biggers, and Homer's mama, Mrs. Prudence Biggers—all free by law."

"Or by forgery, dad gum!" said Will.

James admired the beautiful hand lettering on the rich parchment. He itched to have his sketch-book in his hands again. The image that had haunted his dreams through these fitful days flooded his mind again: the sketchbook pages skipping on the water, then bloating up, sinking into the creek they'd jumped in that first day out in Kentucky. "It's fine work," James said enviously. "We'll be able to get Homer and the women on the steamboat with these papers."

"Fool," Will muttered. "You think it's going to be that easy?"

James felt his hackles rising again. He'd not had the luxury of being mad at Will while every step had felt like a leap into peril, but now that they were only hours away from safety, he allowed the comfortable wave of anger to wash over him. "Person's got to have hope, Will Bowers. Thee's a sour-plum pessimist."

Sabetha and Miz Pru and Callie were delivered to Mrs. Simms's front parlor.

"Chicken livers," Callie said, touching the brocade drapes and every one of Mrs. Simms's glass animals on the tables. "Wish me and Mama and Miz Pru could have stayed here. The place we stayed was just two shades better than a pigsty."

"Was not," Miz Pru said. She couldn't bring herself to sit in the puffed-up chairs, so she lowered her backside to the edge of the piano bench.

Sabetha said, "Notice anything different about Callie?"

There *was* something, but James couldn't put his finger on it. She seemed right clean and a little taller, but there was something else.

Callie sank back into one of the brocade chairs and propped her feet out in front of her on a filigreed ebony table.

Shoes! Big, black, shiny ones covered her bony ankles, and those shoes were tied with leather strings that hung over the sides. She jumped to her feet, making an unholy racket on the inlaid wooden floor.

James looked at the shoes enviously. His own boots had been soaked and dried stiff, and the soles were worn so thin that each step scraped at the pudgy underside of his toes.

All of them were slicked up in fresh clothes for the steamboat trip. Loading up on an ample day's worth of food, they started out again at dusk. Callie stamped her feet. "How *do* people abide these clodhoppers? They pinch me awful bad." She clomped around in those big shoes, raising dust and drawing smiles from the black shopkeepers who swept the sidewalks outside their doors.

One more night, James repeated to himself. One more night on the road, and they'd be safely aboard the steamboat in St. Louis, Missouri. They'd sail into Kansas, where the Negroes would be welcomed by Ma and sent North along the Lane Trail up toward Canada and freedom. One more night.

Chapter Forty-Three
ELDER BROTHER WON'T COME

On Saturday, right after I got my Ronald McDonald curls cut off, Tracy and I went back to talk to Bo Prairie Fire. Rain was pounding the roof of the porch like horses' hooves. A bucket in the corner caught a steady leak. The other residents weren't around to show off their weird clothes. I didn't miss the spooky fox martens.

Mr. Prairie Fire lay on the couch with an army-issue wool blanket pulled up to his chin. We sat on the floor beside him, and Tracy asked how he was feeling. Well, I mean you could tell just by looking at him. He was the color of bilgewater.

"Poorly, can't you see? Elder Brother won't come."

"You have an older brother?" I couldn't imagine anyone older than he.

"What we call the sun. Very powerful god. Dresses in smooth deerskin and red feathers. Travels east to west across the heavens. Goes back under the earth at night."

He coughed, a volcano that began deep in his belly and shook him as if he were a puppet on a string. I hurt all over just watching him. When he caught his breath, he talked in spurts, like a faucet turning on and off. "Won't come. Out today. Too much. Rain. Good for the. Thunder beings."

I had a million questions, but Tracy said we should come back when he was feeling better. "Just one question?" I begged, and she said okay, one. "Mr. Prairie Fire, do you know anything about James Weaver? He was a famous architect from here in Lawrence."

The man shook his head. Silver hair stuck out all around his stained pillow. I wondered what the stains were. I slipped in one more question. "Do you know Faith Cloud?"

His eyes rolled back in his head, which scared me to death. "She's Turkey Clan. Too. Kin to Straight. Feather. Same as me."

"Yes!" I replied.

He rolled on his side and drew his knees up to his chest. "Morrison," he said, his face to the wall.

"Morrison, Mr. Prairie Fire?" I encouraged him while Tracy tugged at my sleeve. The rain kept on pounding.

"Jedediah Morrison. He's the one. Took my home. My Lulu and me. Move to Indian Territory. Some call it—" He'd lost his train of thought, and I finished it for him.

"Oklahoma."

"Sounds right," he said, which brought on

another fit of coughing, Tracy called one of the house managers over to keep an eye on Mr. Prairie Fire, and we thanked him and left. I don't think he even heard us go.

Chapter Forty-Four
March 1857
A PAIR OF CONJURERS

The *Queen of the Delta* ruled the river, beckoning all her loyal subjects aboard. Tickets in hand, James felt relief roll over him like a prairie wind, and homesickness stabbed his heart as he thought about Ma and Pa and Rebecca. Twenty-eight days and twenty-eight treacherous nights had passed since James had last seen his house in Lawrence, where Ma cooked up belly-warming treats and where Miz Lizbet, who'd started this whole journey, had been laid to rest. And now it was First Day, March 30, and they were only minutes away from boarding the boat that would deliver them safely to Wyandotte, Kansas.

James could already feel the crisp white sheets he'd sleep between this night, and the splash of hot water on his face and neck when he'd wash up for dinner. Dinner would be served in a dining room sparkling with crystal lights. Older folks would be dancing half the night away, and Will would find a poker game and set about wooing pretty girls.

James felt the springy wood beneath his boot as

he started up the gangplank with Will Just ahead, Homer carried Miz Pru. Suddenly she started to shake like she was in the grips of a raging fever. "NO! No!" she shouted. "We ain't getting on that boat, not while I'm alive and kicking." And she *was* kicking.

James had to jump out of range; lucky she wasn't wearing Callie's clodhoppers. He was just too tired to put up with one of Miz Pru's fits this close to home. "Sabetha, can thee do something with her?"

Sabetha closed her eyes to gather strength against Miz Pru's relentless tide, then tried to reason with the old woman. "Miz Pru, we've got *free* papers, hear? And paid-for tickets. A nice, clean bed's waiting for you down below on that steamboat. Aren't you about ready to lay down your head and rest to the humming of those engines?"

"No, no, no!" screamed Miz Pru as other passengers stared and walked around their sorry circle.

"Homer, set her down," Sabetha ordered. She reached out for Miz Pru's hand, which was jerked away.

Miz Pru was shrieking, and it took both Homer and Solomon to keep her from flying in the air. "No! You tell 'em, Callie. Tell 'em."

James glanced at Callie. Her big shoes seemed nailed to the gangplank as her body swayed like the river. Her eyes were deep, deep in her head. James sensed that they were turned backward, reading something in her mind. "Callie?" He poked her arm. "Is thee alive, Callie?"

Quietly, the girl said, "Miz Pru's right. We can't go on that boat."

"Cal-LEE," Will whined. "I'm just plain sick of you." The leather toe of Will's crutch was worn to the rough wood, and the last day's journey had been painful and exhausting. "If you had the sense of a possum, you'd keep your mouth shut."

Callie looked up at Will as if seeing him for the first time. "You can't get on that boat, Mr. Will, can't, can't, can't."

"Watch me do it," Will snapped.

"But don't you see? Miz Pru sees it, I see it, why can't you?"

"See what?" James demanded. "What does thee see?"

Callie just shuddered, unable to bring the words out.

"What I see," Will said, "is that you're a superstitious, squirrely girl, ungrateful, too, and Miz Pru's crazy as a loon. That boat sails in half an hour, and I'm sailing with it." He whipped his ticket out of James's hand and hobbled up the gangplank. *Clunk, clunk*—the crutch's footsteps echoed all around.

James started after him, but Solomon stopped him with a firm grip. "Mr. James, we'd best listen to Miz Pru."

James swallowed ripples of anger as Will vanished inside the boat. Its engine was churning away here where the Mississippi and the Missouri pooled together. Minutes ago the water had seemed calm and welcoming. Now waves splashed against the body of the boat as the huge side-wheels spun in torrents of violent water.

Miz Pru insisted they wait along the riverbank until *it* happened, and it happened only minutes after leaving port. A cosmic burst of fireworks lit up the sky like the most spectacular Fourth of July James had ever witnessed. At the same time, the ground moved as if some huge dragon had burrowed through the earth just beneath James's body.

Someone yelled, "Holy Jesus God, the boiler must have blown!"

Screams from the river chilled James to the marrow as pillars of fire darted into the air. The night sky turned midday bright. No one on the boat survived the fire.

Chapter Forty-Five
HOLLYWOOD EXTRAVAGANZA

Mike in a tie! It must have been one of his father's, because it hung just below his belt. He's at that awkward age: too tall for clip-ons and too short for normal ties. But I have to admit, he looked kind of cute.

In all modesty, I have to say I knocked his socks off. His *white* socks. My hair looked very chic and straight, for a change, because it was too short to spring into clown curls. And I wore a new black dress, one that fit. My dad just shook his head when he saw how closely it fit and how much skin showed above and below the dress.

My mom said, "Don't get nervous, Jeffrey. The dress is long enough to cover the subject and short enough to be interesting."

"A little *too* interesting," Dad said.

Mike, of course, nearly lost his lunch when he saw me, because until that night he'd thought of me as a genetically impaired boy. He swallowed a few times and stammered something about Howie and the Bubble-Head waiting in the car.

Mom and Dad gave me the usual pep talk:

"Make sure you've got a flashlight in the car and the spare's in good shape," Dad said, to which Mom added, "Don't eat meat or fish that's not cooked through."

"Absolutely no alcohol."

"Remember, don't dance too vigorously on a full stomach; let your food settle."

"Honey, don't forget you're allergic to geraniums."

Finally they ran out of warnings and said, "Have a good time." Oh, right. It was like going out on leave from the army. Just as we were getting into Howie's car, Mom called from the porch, "Oh, and Mike, see that she doesn't eat any fire, okay?"

The party was a Hollywood extravaganza. Mike's cousin Sarah, the guest of honor, was an old-movie freak, so we had blown-up pictures of Humphrey Bogart and Claudette Colbert and Cary Grant and Lauren Bacall staring at us from three walls, with black-and-white movie scenes flickering along the fourth. It was like an unending episode of *Dream On.*

We had to present a ticket outside the Doubletree ballroom at this fake box office made out of cardboard, probably a refrigerator box. I pictured Bo Prairie Fire trying to stay warm living in a box like this. Maybe that's why he got so sick.

Then a guy showed us to our assigned table. They had him done up in one of those old Philip Morris usher uniforms with the dorky flat caps held in place by an elastic band under the chin. He looked so miserable in that getup that Mike and I felt sorry for him and snuck fancy morsels out to him from the dessert table.

There were yards of sprocketed film scattered on the tables, and old movie cans held pots of—you guessed it—geraniums. "I'm allergic to geraniums," I reminded Mike as a sneeze crept up on me.

A DJ played tunes from the '30s and '40s for the first hour while we all stuffed our faces on foods from at least six major world cultures, if you count hamburgers and French fries and pizza as cultural experiences.

Everyone seemed to be having a great time, except Sarah. Her red satin dress was so froufrou that she could barely move, and she'd already dropped a hunk of smoked salmon on her chest and had a grease spot that looked like an eye socket.

The DJ began playing music we'd at least heard before—stuff from the '70s and '80s—and it was pretty lively, so everybody just got up and danced in one big mob. Then suddenly the pace slowed, and "Unchained Melody" came blasting over the loud-speaker while James Cagney flickered against the wall in some old prison movie. Mike put his arms around my waist, and I put my arms around his neck, and we sort of rocked from foot to foot in sync while the guy sang, "Oh, my love, my darling, I've hungered for your touch, a long, lonely time."

It was one of those gripping, defining moments that can make or break a relationship. Mike and I were exactly the same height. He smelled so good, and his ears were red the way they get around Celina, the cheerleader, and we swayed to the same rhythm with our arms around each other, and our knees gently knocked every so often, which was thrilling, and what could I do?

I leaned forward and whispered into one of his red ears, "Bo Prairie Fire is a Turkey, you know."

Chapter Forty-Six
April 1857
A DANG GOOD FORGERY

"Will it be mutton, young sir, or would you prefer the poached salmon?" The waiter stood over James, who suspected this was not the first time he'd been asked for his choice. Mutton or salmon—it made no difference. Solomon and the others were in the Negro section of the boat, and James was alone aboard the *Wilmington,* here at this fancy table among seven passengers giddy with wine.

How would he *ever* tell Will's ma? Why hadn't he stopped Will? He could have; he was strong enough now. But his friend was dead, and James could never forgive himself.

He thought back to that first day when he'd seen Will with the empty sack of trousers that a strong leg had once filled. In Will's place, he'd wondered, would he want to live with one good leg and one throbbing phantom limb to remind him of what he'd lost?

But Will *had* wanted to live, and live fiercely.

"The fish is excellent, young sir. Shall I bring the salmon?"

James nodded while the conversation buzzed

around his head like mosquitoes, and the tinkling of glasses made his ears stop up as if he were swimming in deep water.

James was the first one off the boat in Wyandotte, but it was a long wait until the *Wilmington* disgorged its Negro passengers.

Callie joined him on the shore, carrying her shoes. He was so glad to see her, he could have spit into the wind! Homer walked in small circles like a dog marking his territory.

Miz Pru sniffed the fragrant April air and said, "Kansas ain't no Garden of Eden."

"No, ma'am, but it's home," James told her, realizing that Kansas truly was his home now, more so than Boston, where he'd spent the first twelve years of his life.

Solomon herded their group together while James went to hire a coach to carry them to Lawrence. Suddenly he heard Solomon's voice rise above the milling crowd. "Mr. James, you'd best come back."

Solomon had an arm around each of the women, and Homer clutched Callie's hand while a man with a gravelly voice demanded to see their papers. Sabetha's face flushed. Miz Pru had her feet planted wide, and James saw her dress ripple over shaking knees.

He stepped forward. "Pardon me, sir. Is thee an official?"

"What's it to you?"

"These are my friends, sir."

The man glowered at James. "*Thee* are a snotty little kid. Leave me to my business, boy."

James mustered a cordial smile and looked the man full in the eyes. "Might I see thy badge, sir?"

The man's breathing was loose and wheezy as he yanked a leather billfold out of his back pocket. He flipped it open and shoved it up under James's nose. His name was Lonny Brill, from St. Joseph, Missouri.

"I thank thee kindly, sir, but thee is not a U.S. marshal."

James saw a flicker of a smile in Solomon's eyes.

"What I am is a citizen sworn to uphold the law, which says loud and clear that a man has a right to have his stolen property returned. Call me a wild dreamer, but I suspect these folks are runaways. Unless you can prove otherwise," he added, daring Solomon.

Solomon presented his own papers first.

"Uh-huh, sure enough you're a free Negro, in the hire of a Dr. Olney, says here."

"Yes, sir." Solomon sounded calm, but James heard a tremor in his voice.

Lonny Brill slid the other papers on top of Solomon's. Now Sabetha stood behind Miz Pru, locking both the woman's arms in place. Homer tossed his rubber ball from hand to hand; pieces of rubber flaked off onto his scuffed boots. Callie jammed her feet in her shoes and stared straight ahead.

Lonny Brill's eyes flitted across the words. "This doesn't do it, friends."

"But they're *free* papers," Callie cried, before Sabetha could clap her hand across Callie's mouth.

"I suppose you're the girl mentioned here? Callie Biggers?"

"Yes, sir," she mumbled.

"Well, I've got news for you, Callie Biggers. This paper's not worth the ink spilled on it. It's a dang good forgery, that I'll grant you, but it's not the genuine article. You know how I can tell? There's no official seal on this document. There's got to be an official seal. Looks like my buddies and I will just have to return you folks to your owner."

Chapter Forty-Seven
THE DELAWARE PROJECT

If Mike and I had spent half as much time on schoolwork as we were spending on the Delaware Project, we'd be brilliant. Well, we're already brilliant, but not in ways that get you on the honor roll.

Ahn had wanted to come to the University of Kansas library with me and work on this project just as we'd worked together on the mystery of Miz Lizbet's skeleton. I'd wheedled out of it so I could work with Mike. It's true that he has never been a hotshot researcher before, but after we'd had our arms around each other at that party and clunked knees, it was kind of nice to sit in the dark at a blue-screened microfilm reader and exchange Significant Grimaces and Grunts. Love blooms in weird gardens, you know what I mean? That is, if you don't mind a few weeds.

We piled all kinds of Kansas history tomes on the table and rolled over to a microfilm reader to scan the old Lawrence city directories. Next to us was a serious student, a guy in a Kansas City Chiefs ball cap, who fast-forwarded through about thirty rolls while we were figuring out how to load the first one.

Eventually we got it, and rolled and rolled until we found Jedediah Morrison, living on Vermont Avenue, in 1857. Occupation: oculist.

Mike dashed over to the monster dictionary to look up *oculist:* Jedediah made spectacles—eyeglasses, that is—and spyglasses and magnifying lenses. He was listed as a widower with one son, Flint, age thirteen. The same age as James Weaver.

Mike said, "Old Jedediah's not listed in the 1858 directory. Think he died?"

"Or moved suddenly." I dropped three rolls of microfilm, and Chiefs Cap glared at us.

"Bo Prairie Fire had mentioned land up near Leavenworth. I'll check." I scouted out the Leavenworth city directory for 1858. "Here he is." Jedediah Morrison turned out to be on the Leavenworth County tax rolls for the next six years, but in his last year he'd had a walloping increase in his taxes.

"He made a pile of money in 1863, Mike. Maybe he sold his land."

"What land?"

"Good question," I conceded.

"And why in the middle of the Civil War?"

"We've got loads of questions, just no answers," I said with a sigh.

Mike flipped through pages of a pictorial history of Kansas. He kept muttering, "1863 . . . 1863 . . . Nothing special happened."

The man in the Chiefs cap said, "Wrong, kid. That's the year Congress turned over land to build the railroad in Kansas. Right across the Delaware Strip."

I looked at him curiously. Since when was this *his* project? But three heads are better than two, as the saying goes.

Mike began doodling in his notebook. He drew a really awful Conestoga covered wagon with huge wheels. He has this theory that if you scribble swirly circles long enough, something important will start to appear on the paper out of your sheer boredom, so his pencil kept tracing around and around one of those wheels until it cut through the paper, which gave me an idea.

"Look at it this way." I drew an enormous wheel and printed JAMES WEAVER at the hub. "Let's label all the spokes." We came up with ten of them:

(1)   Miz Lizbet
(2)   Mattie and Ray Berk
(3)   Ernie's Bait Shop
(4)   Delaware Indian land
(5)   Faith Cloud
(6)   Jedediah Morrison
(7)   Flint Morrison
(8)   Samuel Straightfeather
(9)   The missing treaty
(10) Bo Prairie Fire

"Who's Bo Prairie Fire?" asked Chiefs Cap.

"An old croupy Indian," Mike explained.

"Delaware?"

"What else?"

I yellow-highlighted each spoke as it fed to the center of our wheel. "Now all we have to do is figure out how each of these is connected to the hub."

"Which is James Weaver, of course," Mike said with a sneer.

I thought about it a minute. "Here's what we know for sure: James knows Flint, and Bo Prairie Fire knows *about* Flint's father, Jedediah Morrison. Also, Straightfeather and Bo and Faith are somehow related."

"Same clan, maybe?"

"Faith tells her dear old neighbor Mattie about a treaty that was written but never ratified, or maybe it was ratified, then lost."

"Or stolen," Chiefs Cap suggested.

Mike said, "Suppose James knows something about Delaware land rights. Say he's friends with an Indian, or his father's the lawyer for some of the Delaware people, and there's a big mess over who owns what land and who's going to sell it to the railroad for a killing. Say James knows about the secret treaty, and he gives his buddy Flint some inside info."

I shook my head. "The James I know wouldn't do anything so sleazy."

"Oh, no, of course not," Mike said. "Saint James Weaver."

By now, Chiefs Cap was practically foaming at the mouth. "A treaty like that would be worth serious money in the hands of the Delaware people, because they'd be entitled to reparations from the U.S. government with about one hundred fifty years' worth of interest. Man, I wish I were on the Delaware rolls."

Mike said, "But, on the other hand, if the treaty doesn't get to the tribe at all and lands in Washington first, it might just accidentally vanish and never resurface, right?"

"Possibly," I said thoughtfully, "but it would also be worth a lot of money if it *never* turned up. Think. If the railroad's going to be built in Kansas, it's got to buy land from somebody, right?"

"Right," Mike agreed. "And the land belongs to the Delaware Indians."

"Or it would, if the treaty ever got ratified," Chiefs Cap added.

Mike began tapping the desk furiously with his pencil. "Oh, man, what if Jedediah Morrison sells Indian land to the railroad?"

"How does he get it?" Suddenly another theory popped into my mind. "James and Flint go to school together. Let's say James knows about the treaty Mr. Prairie Fire was rambling on about. He tells his buddy Flint about the treaty. James wants to make sure it gets into the right hands, like under the nose of a Delaware chief."

Mike finished my thought: "But somebody steals it."

"Flint Morrison!"

"And it's lost forever."

"Until now!" I said, triumphantly.

Chapter Forty-Eight
April 1857
A MORAL DILEMMA

A band tightened around James's chest as he saw panic replace the smile in Solomon's eyes. "These are my kinfolk," Solomon told Lonny Brill. "I'm carrying them to Lawrence to help out the Olneys."

"Good try, Mr. Free Negro Man, but I happen to know that four slaves matching the description of your *kinfolk* have gone missing out of Owensboro, Kentucky. An old lady, oh, I'd say about like this one. A big, strong buck. A young woman, lithe and pretty, and, what do you know, a girl said to be ten or eleven. Can you beat that coincidence?"

James said, "Sir, these people have been traveling with me. I can swear to thee that they're free citizens. Go after my father, please. He's a lawyer in Lawrence. He'll straighten this all out."

"I don't care if he's Jesus walking on water, boy. These are now *my* Negroes, and they are worth a nice stack of dollars." The man pulled out a gun. Homer tugged at Miz Pru's safety rope.

James and the others drew together into a tighter circle. How could they come this close to victory and still lose? James saw that Sabetha was looking for a way to run. He flashed her a warning no!—while his own mind raced through possibilities.

A tall, angular man with a curled mustache stepped forward. "How much are these Negroes worth to you, sir?"

"None of your business, unless you're buying," said Lonny Brill.

"I have a proposition for you." The man tugged at his white cuffs. He wore a wide-brimmed hat stained with sweat, but was otherwise immaculate.

James scanned the man's face; was he a true abolitionist, a Free-Soiler? Or was he offering to pay for the runaways only to sell them to someone else in the South for lots more money?

"Permit me to confer with the young man who appears to be their champion. Hold your fire on these unfortunate wretches, sir, until the boy and I can—shall we say—reach favorable terms?" The man led James aside by the elbow. "I scratch your back, you scratch mine."

"Sir?"

"It's the American way of doing business, son. You have a commodity you wish to preserve, at any cost, am I right? Mr. Brill, there, has a commodity he wishes to possess so he can sell it to the highest bidder. Do you follow me so far?"

"I think so, sir."

"Very good. I, as the third leg of this tripod, have

a document, a certain Delaware land rights treaty, that I wish to misplace until I can raise a little capital. I aim to purchase the land that already belongs to my family—by squatter sovereignty, by God—but that greedy Delaware near-savages claim as their own."

Cringing at those harsh words, James asked, "Might I ask how thee came by this treaty, sir?" He was trying to piece the picture together, but it was all muddled in his mind.

"I happened to be at the unfortunate demise of a certain Bureau of Indian Affairs agent, a man of rectitude and resolve, but alas, he's just as dead today as a man of my own caliber would be under the same circumstances, which is to say, a knife to the heart."

James's stomach tightened with the gasp he held in.

"On the Indian agent's last breath he thrust this document into my hand and entreated me to see it safely to Washington." The man laughed heartily, not at all the response James would expect from someone honoring a deathbed plea.

"Now, I could simply burn this magnificent piece of parchment or watch it turn to pulp in the river. But I'm a good man at heart."

James suspected he was anything *but* good as the man patted his chest in pride. "I trust you're a member of the Society of Friends, as the Quakers call themselves, am I right? Conscientious folk, all of you?"

"Yes, sir."

"Now, understand me, I do not wish to finagle those poor Indians out of their land. I only want my share. I'll build a sweet little house, plant forty acres in corn, and live like the gentleman I was born to be."

"Forgive me, sir, but I can't help wondering why thee's so keen on that plot of land when there's this vast prairie out here and room enough for everyone."

The man looked at him as if he were daft. "Well, you're just a boy. I've got a lad about your age, and he's green as sapling, too. There's going to be a railroad come through here, right across that prime Delaware reserve. Right across *my* land. My very *valuable* land, if you're viewing it through the eyes of the Leavenworth, Pawnee, and Western Railroad."

James swallowed a dry lump in his throat and realized he was no match for this man. If only Will were there. . . .

"Now, I am an excellent judge of character," the man said. He looked James up and down as if he were fitting him for a suit.

"I'm losing my patience," Lonny Brill shouted, waving the pistol he'd kept the runaways in line with.

"We're reaching the end of our negotiations," the man called back, then turned again to James. "I trust you, with all your *thee*s and *thou*s, to hide this

232

document while I raise the money out east to buy a handsome passel of that land."

"But, sir, the land belongs to the Delaware people. The U.S. government moved them out here to Kansas Territory and deeded them that land. My pa's a lawyer. He explained it all to me."

"Quite right, son, until two, three years ago, when the government convinced those poor souls to sell cheap all but a ten-mile-by-forty-mile swath of that land on the north bank of the river. Haven't you heard about the Delaware Strip? Some call it the Delaware Trust Lands?"

"Yes, sir, I've heard those words," James said with a sigh.

"Those fools should have known better than to *trust*," the man said. "One of their chiefs woke up one fine Kansas morning and realized just what they'd given away for mere cents on the dollar, and he called for a new treaty. This piece of paper"—the man patted his breast pocket—"deeds them back a handsome patch of land. My land, I might add. Or, more precisely, it shall be my land as soon as I raise the sizable capital."

"That land, sir, which ought to belong to the Delaware tribe, now's owned by the government?"

"Unless this treaty goes into effect. You see my dilemma. The Delawares, of course, would never sell it to me."

"And the government aims to sell Delaware land right out from under them?"

The man shrugged. "We've all got our price, boy. You, too, I suspect."

What would Will do? Will always had the sure, right word ready to roll off his tongue. James glanced back at the band of his friends, sorely minus Will. All of their lives hung on these words. Callie had her arm around Miz Pru, and Miz Pru's empty eyes darted nervously as she chewed her gums as if they were a wad of tobacco. The spring air hung heavy with expectancy.

He could feel his own will bending. "And what of the treaty, sir?"

The man said, "I'm obliged to misplace the document, you see, because a certain officer of the law suspects it's in my possession. It wouldn't be, if it were in yours. Do you understand?"

James did *not* understand, but he waited to hear more.

"Oh, I suppose I could bury the document in a steel box out on the wild prairie, but somebody might strike it when they were turning sod. Well, a lesser man might take that chance."

"It's a mighty big prairie out there," James reminded the man again. He glanced over and caught Callie's pleading look.

"But, alas," the man was saying, "it's in my best interest not to know where this document rests, should anybody ask me. I'm a gentleman. I would not thrive behind bars, imbibing federal swill. Do I make myself clear, boy?"

"I believe so, sir."

"We have an agreement, then? You promise me to bury the treaty and not let on to a soul?"

"And in return, sir?" The words tasted foul on James's tongue, milk gone sour in the sun.

"In return I pay Mr. Brill, there, the paltry sum he'd get for the Negroes—less his considerable handling expenses—you take the wretches home, and everybody's needs are served."

"Except the Delaware Indians', sir."

"Ah, yes, but in five years' time you'll mail that treaty document to the Bureau of Indian Affairs. You'll swear you've just located it, say, among some tornado rubble. Then the Delaware will get what's coming to them for their trouble, courtesy of Uncle Sam in all his bounty. The railroad will bring the outside world to the prairie. As for me, I will have sold my land to the railroad and will be living in the throes of luxury in a far-off state. I fancy New Hampshire. As I mentioned, everybody's happy."

James bent over, stalling, tugging at his trousers, which were high over his ankles now. Straightening up, he said, "One thing still troubles me, sir, if thee doesn't mind my asking."

The man twisted the diamond studs in his stiff, white cuffs. "Aye?"

"Does thee have so much as a care for these Negroes?"

The man turned his face to the clouds. A thick plum in his throat caught James's eye.

"My boy, I'm a practical man. Money, as they say, is money, and land is land. But even I have moral limits. Buying a man's body and soul to work your land, that's where I draw the line. Can I trust you, boy? Do I have your solemn word?" He twirled the tips of his mustache while his eyes, once playful, now gored James.

James remembered Grandpa Baylor saying, "Son, always remember, a man's word is as solid as a mountain. It can't be bent or splintered or broken."

James had lied or played carelessly with the truth too many times on this trip, but only to save people's lives. Even Ma lied to save lives. Could he give his word to this evil man?

He couldn't abide the thought of *selling* human beings as if they were cattle or wheat. And yet the man's money would release the runaways James had so painfully traveled among these past weeks—sweet Homer; and tiny Miz Pru, padded with turkey feathers; and Sabetha, with her sharp tongue; and Callie, seeing things in her back mind; and Solomon, who'd been his friend ever since he'd come to Kansas. What could he do?

What *would* Will do? What would Ma do, if it came to trading one people's injustice for another's? And what was the alternative?

He looked over at the assembled circle. Lonny Brill stood there with the sun glinting off his revolver and unfurled a length of nasty rope he meant to tie the runaways with.

James saw them each so clearly, so achingly: Solomon, trying to reason with Brill; Miz Pru, with the safety lariat still hanging from her waist, rolling on the balls of her bare feet while Sabetha whispered in her ear and held her in check; Homer, bent over, rocking, clutching his red ball; and Callie, with her snakeskin around her neck, stamping the new grass beneath her shoes and her eyes darting around like a cornered animal's. What if she took off running? She'd be shot in the back!

Suddenly he heard a wail of grief from Homer as his rubber ball made its wobbly roll right toward James. Homer broke free of the circle and rushed after his ball.

"Git back here!" Lonny Brill shouted, and he fired his gun into the air.

"Sweet Jesus, what happened?" Miz Pru cried.

In the confusion, the man slipped the treaty into James's hand just as Homer bent to pick up the rubber ball. He clutched the ball in both hands, lips quivering, and gave James a curious look.

James said, "Thee must get back and look after the others, Homer. Tell them everything will be all right now."

"Then I presume we have a deal?" the man said.

Sick to his soul, James nodded his agreement. He and the tall stranger were in business. Dirty business. The man put out his hand, and James reluctantly shook it as Homer carefully passed his rubber ball from hand to hand.

"Pity we'll never meet again," the man said. "You seem to have promise as a businessman." He strode over to Lonny Brill and opened his billfold.

Chapter Forty-Nine
WHEREAS AND HERETOFORE

I clicked off our microfilm reader, and the shrinking image winked from the center of the screen. Chiefs Cap lost interest in the Delaware and returned to his own research project at another machine.

Mike and I sat back in our big wooden chairs as he whispered, "Ernie's got his shack and the bait shop right on Delaware land and a parrot named after a Delaware chief. What's missing from this picture, Dana?" I shrugged my shoulders.

Mike scooted his chair closer to me. I could smell his Freedent gum as he said, "All Mattie and Ray have to do is get their hands on this mysterious document, sell it to the Indians, and presto, they're filthy rich and can move out of that depressing house with the cat flap door."

"Good thinking!" I squeezed Mike's cheeks together, the way a grandmother does when you've finished all your cauliflower. The gum flew across the table. "Suave, Mike." I picked up the wad with a piece of notebook paper and presented the gift to him. "Now all we have to do is figure out why James had that treaty, how Flint got it—"

"And where it is now," Mike said.

We hit the computers, and a half hour later Mike spread the printout on the library table with the listing of every reference to the Delaware in the library. We scanned through all sorts of entries on death rituals, unwilling removals west and south, exotic clothing of silver and feathers, turtle rattles, Doll Being, Snowboy, Great Bear, matrilineal descent, cedar smoke to cure nightmares, and treaties, treaties, treaties.

Something suddenly popped out at me:

HEARING BEFORE THE SELECT COMMITTEE ON
   INDIAN AFFAIRS
RE: DELAWARE INDIAN JUDGMENT FUNDS

A harried librarian directed us to government documents, which were caverns and mountains of stuffed tan file boxes arranged by month and year. We marched up and down the stacks, blurred dates streaking past us.

"Here it is." Mike pulled down the right box and found the right booklet as flimsy as Christmas wrap, and we buried ourselves in some of the most boring stuff you'd ever want to read. Lots of *whereas*'es and *heretofore*s and *pursuant to*s, but by the end of it we discovered some important facts. Descendants of Kansas Delaware Indians were *still* battling the U.S. government over violations of their land rights going back 150 years. To top that, the government was refusing to recognize the Delaware as a legitimate tribe with legal claims to Kansas land.

"Can you believe this, Dana? The government says the Delaware are just a splinter group of the Cherokee Nation. I'll bet there's not a Delaware alive who thinks *that*."

"Now we've got to get some answers from Bo Prairie Fire." That would be tough, but I hoped he might be thinking more clearly when he got his coughing under control. A swig of that codeine cough medicine Mom stashed in the medicine cabinet might help, if I could spirit it out of the house, or else Faith Cloud's murky, fermented tea.

We actually had our second bed-and-breakfast customers. Their car, with New Mexico plates, was parked at the side of the house. They were probably visiting their kid at KU. Mom was in the kitchen working up to another sour cream coffee cake, the phone clamped between her chin and her shoulder. "For you, Dana. It's that Tracy person."

Tracy had a deep voice, deeper than Mike's. "I have some bad news, Dana. It's about Bo Prairie Fire. He died this morning. Pneumonia."

"Oh, no." My first thought was, *It's not fair. I'm so close to solving the mystery, and he's got the key*. Then I realized how selfish that thought was, and a pang of sadness hit me for this lonely old man. I pictured him wracked with coughing and ranting on about things that made very little sense. Yet all those ramblings might have been just a protective shell for the nugget of truth hidden inside. If only I could get to it. "I'm really sorry, Tracy." Stupid. It wasn't her fault. But it's hard to know what to say in a situation like this. Death is just embarrassing.

"He had no family," Tracy said, "so the shelter called me when he went to the hospital. I'm the only one who's been visiting him for the last few months, besides you." Her voice sounded weary, as if she'd been up all night, and maybe she had. Maybe she'd sat with him at the hospital. Maybe he hadn't died alone.

She continued, "It's really sad that a man lives to be eighty years old and doesn't have any descendants to remember him. Kind of makes me want to get married and have a bunch of kids."

"Uh-huh," I said. I just wanted to get this conversation over with and go up to my room and cry.

Tracy sounded like she was fighting back tears also as she told me, "There's a funeral service Friday. The shelter found a couple of Delaware men from Bartlesville, Oklahoma, to do it right. It's an anthropologist's dream. I'll pick you up a few minutes before noon."

Chapter Fifty
April 1857
LANE'S CHIMNEYS

"I look like a wild woman." Sabetha tried to tame her hair into braids as they neared Lawrence. "Your mama will have one look at me and throw me down the well."

"Not my ma. She's the mildest of women," James lied. It was true that Ma had grown more gentle in his mind with the passing days of travel, but there was no way to prepare these pilgrims for Ma's donkey-stubborn ways. Within two hours of arrival she'd have them all washed and fit and painting the barn and putting up strawberry jam. Why, she was probably already heating up the iron for the bedsheets they'd be pressing, since James had sent a telegram telling her when they'd arrive.

Spring storms had carved great ruts in the road, and James and all the free Negroes bounced along in the coach with the men on one side and the women on the other. Their words sounded jiggly, as if they were talking underwater.

"Anyway, my ma will be so glad to see us, thee could come with ten hairy warts spread across thy face and she'd think thee beautiful." Truth was, they all looked bedraggled. Miz Pru barely weighed as much as a spring lamb now. Solomon's clothes hung on him, also, and his eyes had sunk into dark, baggy circles. Callie's legs and arms were scarred and tracked with red welts—flea bites, probably, since it was too early for mosquitoes. Homer's hair was as wide as a hatbox. Pa would want to take hedge clippers to it. And no telling what James himself looked like, with his britches three inches above his ankles and his coppery hair spread out over his shoulders like a girl's.

Sabetha said, "I've been hearing Lawrence, Lawrence, Lawrence since we left Bullocks'. What's it like, anyway?"

How do you describe where you come from? "It depends on where you're standing," James explained. "Now, Free-Staters like my pa say it's the Athens of Kansas." Sabetha looked puzzled. "Athens is a big city with all kinds of wonderful old buildings. It's in Greece, in Europe."

"Well, I knew that," Sabetha snapped.

"But those proslavery people, they can't tolerate Lawrence being organized as a free-soil town. They say it's the Gall Bag of the Territories."

Miz Pru dozed, and each time she woke, she took up the conversation right where she'd left off. "I say, it's been one devil of a trip, one devil. But, next stop we're at freedom's door."

"Yes, suh! Soon be free!" Homer said.

Solomon stirred uneasily. "Miz Pru, there's something you don't know."

"I've lived twice as long as you, Solomon Jefferson, each day knowin' troubles. Honey, don't I know it all."

"Yes, ma'am, but I've lived in Kansas, and you haven't, not yet. Slave catchers once came for me over in Olneys' front yard, Miz Pru."

"You don't say?"

"Yes, ma'am. Took me with them. I'd have been dragged after a horse hadn't been for Mr. James's daddy."

Sabetha shot Solomon a killing look. "You been lying to us all this way, filling our heads with talk of being home free? If that's true, you're about the cruelest man on the earth, crueler than any master in Kentucky."

James tried to rescue Solomon. "No more lies, Sabetha." Except the big one, about the Delaware Indians, which he'd keep to himself. "We've still got to hide thee out, but thee can stay safe in our house until my pa can fix the legal papers, official seal and all. When thee's good and ready, we'll pass thee North with all thee needs for safe passage."

"Will it be dangerous?" Callie's voice was weary; since they'd lost Will, she'd aged years.

"Not as dangerous as what we've been through, I promise thee, but it's not a glory trip, either. Or

245

thee could take thy chances and make thy home in Lawrence."

Sabetha pinned the last of her braids in the crown around her head. "Well, at least *somebody's* telling us the way it truly is."

Solomon lowered his head almost to his knees, pierced by Sabetha's poison-arrow words, until she poked him with her toe. "Oh, don't look so hangdog."

"Will—" Just the mention of his name made James's throat tighten. Before long he'd have to sit with Will's grieving ma. "Will made thee a map to follow out of Topeka, along the Lane Trail, up through Nebraska Territory, and all the way north to Canada."

"You comin' with us, Mistuh James, suh?"

James took a deep breath. "No, Homer, I'm staying here with my family; thee must go with thine."

They were silent for a time, except for Miz Pru's snores and the rattles of the coach. Miz Pru woke again. "And how we gonna know the right way to go?"

"The Underground Railroad operates all up and down the Lane Trail. Will said thee's to look for piles of stones across each valley. Thee can see them from one peak to the next. They're called Lane's Chimneys, and they tell thee the right direction to safe houses and such."

"How do we know Mr. Will's right?" Sabetha asked. "The boy's dead as a tree stump."

"Will's made the trip more than once. Thee must trust his word." As James said this, he realized that he was no longer a person to be trusted, for he'd made a deal with the devil. He could never tell Ma. He'd hide that treaty document so well that even if she turned the house inside out for spring cleaning, she'd never find it. Never.

"James Weaver, is that thee? Why, thee's grown a country mile, son." Ma embraced him briefly. When he'd left, his head had come to her nose. Now, just four weeks later, they met nearly eye-to-eye. She gathered a fistful of his stringy hair. "Lucky Mr. Draper's just sharpened my barber shears. Solomon Jefferson, good to see thee."

Trembles studied James a minute. Assured that he was the same boy, she swished by and curled her tail around his leg.

As James introduced the guests, Ma looked each over, assessing the damage. She handed Callie a wet washcloth and motioned for her to wash the grime off her face and remove that snakeskin around her neck. She lowered Miz Pru into her own rocking chair with the red-and-yellow flouncy cushion. She placed a bowl of peas in her lap. Without missing a beat, Miz Pru began snapping those peas and tossing them into a second bowl. *Clink, clink.* Sabetha was given a half-hemmed flour sack with a needle and thread stuck in it.

"Thee must be hungry as magpies. Thee might also welcome some cool springwater." She passed Solomon a bucket to take to the well out back and handed James a bread knife and Homer a butter paddle. Homer stuffed the rubber ball under his arm and set to the task of smearing fresh-churned butter on thick slices of Ma's rye bread, still warm. James watched him lick his lips in anticipation.

Ma conducted this well-tuned orchestra until she noticed who was missing. Her eyes met James's. "Will's gone home to his mother?" she asked, almost pleading. James shook his head. Ma pressed both hands to her lips; tears filled the corners of her eyes. She closed her eyes in prayer as Sabetha sat with the needle poised in midair, and Homer shifted from foot to foot, snowing bits of his ball.

After the longest time, Ma said, "Sabetha, see to the rabbit stew simmering on the stove. Homer, I believe thee will find a rubber ball in that basket at thy feet. Thine will have to go in the trash bin." To James's shock, Homer turned his crumbling ball over to Ma and gleefully took up Rebecca's blue one that still had some bounce to it. Ma said, "Friends, my husband, Mr. Caleb Weaver, will be home shortly with our daughter. Thee will be perfectly safe here with Solomon whilst James and I are gone."

He'd just gotten home after weeks and weeks of travel; he didn't want to go anywhere, especially not *there*.

"James, thee must tell me about thy friend Will, and then thee and I shall go to Mrs. Bowers and remind her that the Lord has taken Will for a purpose. Thee has four blocks to think how to put that purpose in words, son."

Chapter Fifty-One
THE MISSING TREATY

I did not expect to see Mr. Prairie Fire at his funeral. Well, I knew he'd be there, but I thought the casket would be decently closed as it had been at the only other funeral I ever attended, which was for Grammy Shannon. But when we got to the graveside, there was Mr. Bo Prairie Fire, in full glory.

Two Delaware men had washed and tended the body for two days and had draped him in a white shroud. He lay there facing west, according to custom, and believe me, he never looked so good. Gone were the lines in his forehead, the furrows that had formed when he was wracked with coughing.

Since burial had to be done at high noon, I took two hours off of school, but I couldn't ask my friends to do that. So, we mourners were a pitifully small group: the two Delaware men; Tracy and me; the social worker from the shelter; and the woman who wasn't Lulu. We made a sad half-circle around the coffin and watched silently as one of the Indians carved a notch in the side of the casket for Mr. Prairie Fire's spirit to escape. His spirit was to remain on earth for four days after burial. The older Indian explained in a singsong fashion, half in English and half in Lenape, that on the fourth day he and his son would come back and build a fire to allow Mr. Prairie Fire's spirit to waft to heaven in the smoke of the cedar limbs.

The younger Indian was obviously an apprentice watching every move the master craftsman made, as if someday this solemn task would fall to him and to his own sons. On a silent signal the young man placed a great eagle feather in Mr. Prairie Fire's hands. There were no songs or prayers out loud, but the two Delaware men seemed to be praying silently, as Quakers do.

Tracy, the wanna-be anthropologist, was fascinated by the whole ceremony, but after about fifteen minutes I couldn't bear the tense silence any longer, or Mr. Prairie Fire's lifeless face. I stepped forward over the lumpy grass to study the depth of his grave, which was lined with bark and leaves.

What year is it, Mr. Prairie Fire? I silently asked. The older Indian gave a nod, and, as the grave diggers closed the casket and lowered it into the ground, I heard Mr. Prairie Fire's voiceless reply: "Why, it's *this* year, girlie, eighteen and fifty-seven."

The thud of dry earth on the top of his simple pine box was deeply chilling, and for the first time in my life I realized how utterly permanent death is. Despite the hole in the casket that set his spirit free,

Mr. Prairie Fire's body would wither and decay in the cold, damp earth, and his life would be a flickering memory entrusted to only the few of us on the edge of his grave.

Months before, Jeep and Mike, Sally and Ahn and I had had a sort-of funeral for Miz Lizbet, but we'd never actually known her in the flesh. Mr. Prairie Fire had been alive to me. His voice, his rambling, raspy words, were seared into my memory.

The old Indian said, "We leave Elder Brother to his rest," and we all turned our backs on Mr. Bo Prairie Fire, deep and alone in that hole. Then the young Indian reached into a beautiful basket and pulled out a bundle wrapped in cowhide. "His only treasure," he said as he presented this gift to "Lulu," who was the closest thing to Mr. Prairie Fire's widow. She shook her head and passed it on to me, saying, "Leave it in the hands of the young." Her gray hair flowed down her back and around her face, sopping up tears.

I held the brittle cowhide package and felt Mr. Prairie Fire's spirit pass through me until I swayed like tallgrass in the prairie wind.

Mike was there when I got home, and he surveyed the cowhide bundle that had belonged to Bo Prairie Fire. It crackled with age. I was afraid it would snap like a taco shell as I unfolded it so carefully.

Inside was a dish towel wrapped and wrapped around something as light as air. The edge of the linen dish towel was embroidered with a mono-gram. I ran my finger over the delicate pink thread: MWB.

"Be careful. It's really old," Tracy said, with awe in her voice.

Mike said, "Just open the thing!"

But I couldn't. There was something floating here just beneath the surface of my memory. MWB. I'd seen those initials before, engraved on the jour-nal that had made Miz Lizbet come alive for me. My heart felt like a woodpecker had attacked it, and I was sure Mike and Tracy could hear it knocking. "Do you recognize this, Mike? *W* for Weaver, *M* for Millicent, and *B* for Baylor."

Millicent Baylor Weaver, James's mother!

Mike caught on, and the blood drained from his face. "It's hers, isn't it?"

We gently unfolded the yellowed parchment inside, and there it was, the treaty between the United States government and the Delaware Tribe of Indians. Chief Tonganoxie had signed his name beside the signature of the Indian agent, and both had signed the date: March 26, 1857.

It was time to clue my parents in on what was happening.

※   ※   ※

Dad hurried right home to see the document. "It's genuine, all right," he confirmed. His face glowed with excitement, and Mom beamed, too.

Mike said, "Dr. Shannon, we think this document is what Mr. and Mrs. Berk were looking for when they tore up your bathroom."

"Don't spin out of orbit, Mom and Dad, but I sort of snooped around their room."

"Dana!" Mom cried.

"I know, I know, it's not good for business, and I promise I won't do it to every guest who stays at our B and B. But the snooping paid off."

"What did you find?" Dad asked. The history professor half was winning out over the father half.

"A blueprint of our house and a rare old book by Samuel Straightfeather that's supposed to tell all about this treaty. But the book's gone now." My parents listened. They were great at crunch times like this, so I continued. "Okay, here's the deal, and don't yell until I've finished the whole thing. Mike's brother Howie drove us to Kansas City, and we tried to get into the Berks' house while they're stuck in jail, but we didn't get any farther than the cat door."

Mom clunked her forehead and groaned, but Dad's eyes just glistened.

"Then we met their neighbor Faith Cloud, who's a Delaware, and she's related to poor Mr. Bo Prairie Fire, the man who died."

254

"It wasn't murder, Dr. and Mrs. Shannon," Mike assured them.

"Mom, Dad, I think Faith Cloud's our only hope of solving the whole mystery of the missing treaty."

Dad nodded and went for his car keys.

Chapter Fifty-Two
April 1857
STUNG BY THE LOVE BUG

Mrs. Bowers was tending her vegetables when James and Ma approached. She didn't hear them. James took this as a sign that they should turn back, but Ma dug three fingers into his back and urged him forward.

"Mrs. Bowers?" His voice wobbled.

Glancing around, her soft, doughy face turned to smiles. "Why, if it isn't James Weaver!" She pulled herself to her feet, with Ma's help. "Where's that scoundrel son of mine? Hiding behind some bushes? Will Bowers, show your ugly face. You can't scare me."

Ma said, "Marian, let's go inside."

"Sure enough he'll just pop up at a window and stop my heart. I tell you, that boy's just like his father."

Ma guided Mrs. Bowers into her keeping room, called that because it was the room with the fireplace where the family kept warm in the evenings. James prayed that Will's little sisters wouldn't come around while he told Mrs. Bowers what he couldn't imagine telling her.

"Glass of lemonade, James? I can't wait to hear

about your adventures out east. Did my Will clobber some of those nasty slave catchers? He's got a temper, that one. Tell me before he comes in here boasting like a shameless preacher."

The smile faded from her face as James said, "Mrs. Bowers, Will isn't coming home."

Ma sidled up next to the woman. "He gave his life for an important principle, Marian. I trust that will give thee some comfort."

"Comfort?" she said absently. "Why should that comfort me?"

James perched on the edge of a footstool. "Mrs. Bowers, we wouldn't be here, Solomon Jefferson and the four freed people and myself, if it weren't for thy son Will. He knew things about the traveling that Solomon and I wouldn't have figured out in a dozen years. He made us maps, caught us turtles with his bare hands. We'd still be trying to cross the Ohio River back in Kentucky if it wasn't for Will knowing how to make watertight rafts out of pure nothing." This wasn't completely true, but James deemed a small stretch of the story fitting at this sorrowful time. "Thy son Will stood up to slave catchers and mean-hearted men all along the way and never flinched. He didn't have a scared bone in his body."

Mrs. Bowers's chin and neck seemed to sink into her shoulders. James looked away as two impossibly heavy teardrops etched her cheeks. Finally, she said, "It wasn't enough to get a leg shot off?"

"Does thee want the whole story, Marian?"

"No, none of it." She wiped the tears with her sleeves. "Everett will want to hear about it, no doubt. I'll send him down later. As for me, I'd like to just sit here."

Ma nodded and held her hand.

"Alone."

On the way home, it occurred to James that Mrs. Bowers must hate him for surviving the trip while Will's charred remains floated to the bottom of the Mississippi River. It was another terrible trade: Will's life for his, same as trading the Negroes' lives for the Delawares'.

Was growing up and being responsible always going to be like this? Did every important choice for the good hurt someone else? Open one door, and another one slams in the wind on someone you love?

Ma walked beside him silently. She had such a clear vision of what was good and what wasn't, and if she doubted for even an instant, prayer cleared it all up. For James, important things were always fuzzy, like a shimmery image floating on the horizon. Only houses and buildings came into sharp focus—wood and stone and brick. And none of that murky, fishy isinglass, no. His houses would have genuine, crystal-clear glass that wrapped around the building. Doors out of glass, yes! A house flooded with sunlight. And what *couldn't* you do with native stones carved to fit together like a hand in a glove?

His face suddenly flushed with shame. Will. The Bowers family's grief—that's what he should be thinking about, not mortar and brick. And then, to his further shame, Ma spoke at last. Her voice was husky, the way it got when she'd been praying silently for a long time. She said, "I am proud of thee, son, and so grateful that thee has come home to us safely."

Homer couldn't wait to spill the news: "Mistuh James, suh, we gettin' married!"

"Thee and Sabetha?" *It can't be.*

Solomon said, "Sabetha and me, we've made a pledge to each other."

Callie was ready to pop, but neither Solomon nor Sabetha looked like they'd been stung by the love bug. Miz Pru sat in the rocker with her hands under her, as if they'd take off on their own if she didn't pin them down.

"We gettin' married!"

"All of thee?" Ma asked. "Would somebody say plainly what's going on?"

"Miz Weaver, ma'am," began Solomon, but Sabetha waved the wooden spoon to hush him. "The plain truth is, we just can't keep on going all the way to Canada. We're all tired. Tired of being on the road, tired of having no place to hang out our wash, tired of having no home that's ours; always somebody else's. Look at Miz Pru. She's worn thin as a bed-sheet. So, we all decided it. We're staying here."

"Here?" Ma asked, pointing to her kitchen floor.

"Nearby here," Solomon explained, "if Mr. Weaver can get all these folks free papers nobody's got to worry over."

"He can," Ma assured them, "although with this new Dred Scott decision, thy safety is less certain, even with legal papers."

"I ain't have any dread." Miz Pru freed up one of her hands to shake a finger at James. "You done told us we could take our chances in Kansas, boy, and that's what we're gonna do. This place gonna be awright. Me and Callie knows it, right, girl?" Her elbow jabbed Callie at the waist, and Callie nearly doubled over as she blurted out, "Natcherly."

Sabetha gave the stew another stir and hung the wood spoon in the notch of the kettle. "Miz Pru thinks Solomon needs a wife."

"And thee?" Ma asked.

"Lord knows, I don't need no man." She shot Solomon a playful look over her shoulder.

"Homer and I are going to build us all a house," Solomon said.

"I'll draw thee a house to build, Solomon. I've got a pack of ideas racing round in my head." Blue shutters that folded over the windows at night . . . a sleeping porch with window seats you could flip open like a trunk . . . walls deep enough to build drawers right into them. He could see it all clearly, the way Callie saw happenings in the future.

Sabetha folded her arms across her chest in her usual way. "We'll make a good life here, me and Callie and Homer and Miz Pru. We've all gotten used to Solomon Jefferson."

Solomon smiled and reached out for Sabetha, but Miz Pru, in her uncanny way, sensed the movement and hopped out of her chair to bat his hand away. "Whatchu puttin' your arms aroun'? She ain't your wife yet." Dropping back down into the rocker, she muttered, "Man get milk for free, he ain't gonna buy the cow."

Ma hid a smile and looked from bride to groom. "Does thee love one another?"

They both considered the question, but Sabetha was the first to answer. "Seems to me Solomon's never gonna be done with Lizbet."

His face went the color of limestone at the mention of her name.

Ma nodded. "Quite a remarkable woman, Elizabeth Charles."

"You tellin' me? I done give her life. Now, Sabetha, here, she's my daughter, too; I been carryin' her since she was ten. She's awright."

"Sabetha, does thee love Solomon?"

"Well as I can."

"Love grows. When Mr. Weaver and I first took

our wedding vows, we were like cat and dog. He was quite a contrary man."

He was contrary? Ma couldn't have been a dandelion blowing in the wind, either. Ma was like those giant sunflowers that poked up straight on sturdy stalks and stubbornly turned their faces to the sun. James thought about Callie's question, how his ma and pa ever got together, what with her being all about praying over things, and him being all about proving them.

"We still have our differences now and again, as James will tell thee."

"That's the truth!"

"Callie, does thee approve of this match?" asked Ma.

Callie put her hands on her hips and looked up to Solomon like he was a tall building. "You say we're going to have a house?" He nodded. "You say I'm going to go to school?" He nodded again. "You say we're going to be free folks, no more worrying about people snatching us back to Kentucky?"

"I believe that's true, Callie."

She closed one eye to sight him better, or maybe to scare him, since she'd already proved that she had second sight. "You say you can take care of us, all of us?"

"Try my best," Solomon assured her.

Callie shrugged. "He can marry us."

Ma gave her blessing, too, in a word. "Fine. Now, Sabetha, Mrs. Noonan will be needing help. Her time's coming soon, and Dr. Olney believes she's carrying twins, plus she's got three little ones not yet off to school. Mr. Noonan's the banker. They'll pay a good wage. Homer, what is thy strength?"

"I kin lift a wagon fulla hogs, Miz Weavuh."

Miz Pru said, "My boy Homer's awful good with hounds."

"Yes, suh! They's mush in my hands."

"Otis Clement keeps cowherd dogs. I believe he can use a hand, since his boy's gone off to college in St. Louis. Callie, there's school over at the African church. I dream of a time when all children, black ones and white ones and Indian children, too, can go to school together here in Kansas. Maybe when the territory becomes a state," Ma said, sighing. She cracked a bunch of eggs into a blue crock full of flour. "I'm about to drop these dumplings into the stew. How long since thee's had a steaming bowl of rabbit stew, friends?"

"Oh, 'bout thirty years," said Miz Pru.

"James, you know where the forks and knives are. Won't thy father and sister be surprised to see how many of us will be thanking the Lord for our bread tonight?"

"We're grateful to you, Miz Weaver," Sabetha said.

"Nonsense." Ma curled her lip at the snarl of braids on top of Sabetha's head. "I believe with a little cleaning up, thee shall be a presentable bride. Solomon, could thee kindly go down to the cellar for some spiced peaches? Callie, plates are on the second shelf over there. The peas, Miss Pru?" No one moved. "Well? Are thee all rooted where thee's planted? Handsome meals like this don't happen with a flick of the wrist."

Suddenly everyone was in motion, and Ma whispered to James, "It's a joy to have these people here, but oh, mercy, does my heart weigh heavy for poor Marian Bowers this night."

Chapter Fifty-Three
TIME AND MOTHER EARTH

"I was so surprised when you phoned, kiddos. Days pass, and my phone doesn't ring. Who's this you brought me?" Faith Cloud batted her eyelashes at Dad.

He smiled. "I'm Jeffrey Shannon, Dana's father."

"Married? Poor Faith has no luck at all. Say, you must be Mattie Berk's brother."

I spoke up quickly. "We didn't exactly tell the truth when we were here before. I'm not, strictly speaking, Mattie's niece."

Faith eyed me suspiciously. "I see. No, I don't see at all. Well, I'll bring some iced tea."

"No!" Mike nearly shouted it. "I mean, no, thank you."

Wolf came loping into the room and did a search-and-destroy number with his tail, overturning pots of dried-up plants all over the studio.

"Oh, don't mind the pup," Faith said, setting the pots upright. "He's staying with me for a while. Kitty, too. Mattie and Ray decided to take a little vacation in Mexico."

Mike punched my knee in one of his more subtle moves that said, *Oh yeah?*

"Ms. Cloud," I began.

"Oh, kiddo, everybody calls me Faith. Even I do."

"Okay. We need to ask you a couple of questions. Can you tell us about Chief Tonganoxie?"

"Oh, he was one of the great ones. We had a lot of honored chiefs in the olden days, not just one like a king, like some tribes do. Let's see, around Tonganoxie's time there was Chief Fall Leaf and Chief Sarcoxie and Chief Neconheson and Chief White Turkey, and Chief Journeycake, but he was a *schwonnah*."

"A what?" Mike asked.

"*Schwonnah*. Somebody who goes to the white man's church. He was only half Indian, on his daddy's side, which doesn't count, and a Christian, to boot."

Dad asked, "Do your people still own any land around Leavenworth?"

Faith wrinkled her lips up as if she'd just tasted some bad fish. "Not since 1866, when they kicked us out. Oh, a few stubborn ones stayed in Kansas, about twenty grown folks and twice as many children. But most of us were shipped off to Oklahoma like no more than sticks of furniture. Sold us off to the Cherokee."

"You're still here," Mike pointed out, yanking his foot out from under Wolf's belly.

"You bet." Faith crossed her ankles and leaned her

weight on the sides of her fuzzy slippers. "We folks, the descendants of those brave ones who refused to go, we never got what's coming to us. And now look at that land. It's got cities and oil wells and a busy harbor and gambling casinos—and hardly a tree still standing. Why, I could be rich as the Queen of England today, wearing ugly hats and waving in gloves, if I'd gotten what was mine. At least I'd know nobody was digging up my ancestors to build a high-rise office building. You wouldn't want your folks dug up, would you, for a glass tower?"

"I certainly would not," Dad agreed. He loves dead things. He can spend a whole weekend in an old cemetery and never feel a chill up his spine.

Mike flashed me threatening looks that said, *Either you tell her nicely, or I'll drop the bomb,* so I said, "Faith, we've got some unhappy news. Mattie and Ray aren't in Mexico. They're in the Douglas County jail."

"Jail? Oh, my." She locked her pudgy fingers together. Her nails were painted a sparkly green.

Mike said, "We think they stole your Samuel Straightfeather book."

Faith turned her hands over and over as if she were washing them.

I added, "And we think they're looking for a treaty that was made with your people a long time ago, one that got lost and was never put into law."

Faith shook her head sadly. "I wondered why they asked me so dang many questions."

I said, "They were probably planning to sell the treaty to Delaware descendants in Oklahoma. It would be pretty valuable, don't you think, Dad?" He nodded.

Faith laid her head on her shoulder. Her round face was suddenly lined, as if sadness had painted in the creases. Wolf sensed a change in atmosphere, for his tail stopped swishing and clunked to the floor.

"Another thing, Faith," I began. "You know Bo Prairie Fire?"

"That old loon? We're the same clan, Turkey Clan, but that doesn't mean we're *all* crazy."

"Faith, I hate to tell you this, but Mr. Prairie Fire died a couple days ago. I saw him Tuesday, and he said to say hello to you." It was a white lie, but it would make her feel better while we were delivering one jab after another.

"Poor old sweetcakes," Faith said mournfully. "He hasn't been *right* since 1975, when his wife died. To tell you the truth, he was a few bricks short of a load even before Lulu died. Lulu and Bo and I, we were about the last ones of our clan left in Kansas. Now Lulu's gone, and Bo, too."

Wolf mourned along with Faith. He lay on his back with his legs sticking straight up, and he whimpered while Dad scratched his pink belly.

Faith said, "I always thought Bo had it, that treaty thing everybody's looking for."

I caught my breath and tried not to gallop into

the next question. "Why did you think that, Faith?"

She looked back in time, her eyes fixed on a knot in the wall. "Right after Lulu croaked, he started boasting about it. Nobody paid him any mind. He said Samuel Straightfeather told him about that treaty thing. But anybody who's not drunk or crouching in a padded cell could tell you that old Sam died a hundred years ago. Bo and that man never walked one day on this earth together."

Wolf rolled over and jumped to his feet, as if he'd sniffed a squirrel. "Settle down, pup," Faith said, hurling one ankle over Wolf's back. "Of course, some of our folks believe you can talk to the spirits of our ancestors if Time and Mother Earth are just right for it. Maybe he did, old Bo Prairie Fire. Maybe long-time-ago Sam told him just where that paper was and said for him to hold on to it so it didn't fall into the hands of crooks in the tribe."

"Crooks?" Mike asked.

"Yes, kiddos, even your own can turn against you, if your eyes aren't wide open." She pinched her nose, obviously to keep back tears. "More likely, the old loon just forgot he had it, or didn't even know it. He probably thought he was carrying some gift from the ancestors, and he'd haul it around until he was buried with it."

"We found it," I said quietly.

"Tell the truth? Why, that crazy old turtle! Whatchu gonna do with it, kiddos?"

"Send it to Washington, I guess. What other choice do we have?"

"Why, you could send it to young Chief Ketchum," Faith said. She stared at the knot on the wall again, looking back into a different time and space. "Honest to God, we all suspected Bo's great-great-grandfather had that thing hidden away. He was a white man, doncha know. Only reason he didn't burn it up and throw it back to the earth was because he was married to one of our own. Poor thing died young, birthing her first. I guess the greedy old stag figured his kid would be covered either way, white or Indian, if that thing ever turned up."

It was a long shot, but I asked, anyway. "Do you remember the greedy old stag's name, Faith?"

"Well, sure I do, clear as winter air. Jedediah Morrison, he was. A glass grinder. Bo Prairie Fire's great-great-grandfather."

Chapter Fifty-Four
April 1857
SHEEP IN WOLF'S CLOTHING

The shrill, quick yip of wolves kept James awake on his pallet in front of the dying fire. Beside him, Rebecca made mewling noises in her sleep. James couldn't find a comfortable position free of Rebecca's chimpanzee kicks. He'd looked forward to sleeping in his own bed, but after Solomon went home to Olneys', Ma had sent Homer to James's room, and the three women to Rebecca's.

Wolves. They said a wolf could bite right through the ropes that held a horse to a tree, but if a man came near, that sorry wolf would turn and run. James didn't like thinking of himself as a sorry wolf, or, as Ma said, a wolf in sheep's clothing. But he'd done something shameful, selling out the Delaware people for his own friends, and now he was turning and running, too much of a coward to go back on his word.

Well, wasn't a man's word worth more than the air it took to carry it? A mountain, Grandpa Baylor said, a man's word was a mountain that couldn't be bent or splintered.

And Callie and the others: Didn't their lives have

as much worth as anybody else's? James was pledged to protect them, as he had through the long weeks back and forth across the country. He owed that much to Will and to Miz Lizbet, who, like Moses, hadn't lived to see the promised land. Then he remembered a passage from Isaiah, which Ma used to quote back when Miz Lizbet had first arrived and sent them all spinning: "Hide the outcasts; betray not him that wandereth."

Yet the Delaware were wanderers, too, uprooted from their first home out east and pushed westward mile by mile.

Which way was *right?* Both were, and neither was. James's head reeled. He just had to wake Ma and Pa and talk it out with them.

Upstairs, he inched their door open. The moon highlighted two round forms on the high feather bed. They were turned toward James. Pa's hair was spread across the pillow, and Ma, in her nightcap, fit snug around Pa's back with her face nuzzled into his neck. It was so achingly sweet that James couldn't bear to disturb them.

He'd have to work things out in his own mind, like a grown person.

It must be midnight, James thought. The moon hung high in the sky, lit so bright that James could barely make out the drinking gourd. A sure breeze cut through the slats of the porch, where he sat wrapped in Ma's shawl. Mercy, if anybody saw him, he'd be mortified.

An hour passed, maybe more. The only sounds in the night were the distant wolves and the rustling leaves. After all the traveling, James had become a night person, more apt to be sleepy in the daytime and alert in the dark. He thought and he thought, until he knew what he had to do.

These past weeks he'd learned to pad around silently in the dark, ever vigilant. Inside the house he gathered up everything he needed. He wrapped the Delaware treaty into one of Ma's embroidered flour-sack tea towels, and rolled that up in a swatch of soft cowhide she used as a trivet on the table. He took the shovel Pa kept in a corner by the door and slipped quietly outside.

Around the back of the house, James dug a hole, remembering how he and Pa had buried a few of their treasures during the raid of Lawrence only a few months earlier.

He laid the cowhide roll in the earth and shoveled dirt back over it. He tamped down the mound of newly turned soil and went back into the house. In the drawer of the hutch was the second sketchbook Ma had brought back from Boston, and now he ran his fingers over the raised gold letters on the cover: JAMES BAYLOR WEAVER, KANSAS TERRITORY, 1857.

Crouched by the window, he worked by the light of the moon, sketching the house where everyone but he now slept. It took him two hours and four pencils to finish the sketch, and every muscle ached with tension. Printed on the south elevation of the house, in letters so small that they appeared to be shading unless you looked very closely or had high-powered spectacles, was this message:

> I, James Baylor Weaver, swear to be a man of my word. If the Lord should take me before April of 1862, I ask that thee go out behind the house thee sees here, twenty boot-lengths from the back door, and find buried an unratified treaty with the Delaware Indians of Kansas Territory. Trust that I hid this document for good reason. Send it to the Delaware people and let every man have what's coming to him.

Relieved, James slid under his comforter and fell right to sleep, with Trembles purring on his back.

Months passed. Miz Pru put some meat on her bones, and Homer weaned his first litter of German shepherds. Callie became the best customer of the new Lawrence lending library, the first one in Kansas.

"Thee must stop calling me 'Mr. James,'" he told Callie one day. "Thee's not anybody's servant."

"Well, I thought you'd never say it!" Callie stamped her foot like she always used to. Only now she had dainty girlish shoes with a satin bow that tied at the top of each foot. Every time James saw them, he thought about those gingham napkins Homer had tied over Callie's feet so she'd not stick to the ice on the Ohio River.

Solomon kept working with Dr. Olney and turned into a kind of doctor himself, using a combination of Dr. Olney's remedies and Miz Pru's concoctions to treat most of the black people in Lawrence. "I ain't had to give up my art," Miz Pru said. "Just moved it north."

James filled up his sketchbook, and his proudest accomplishment was the set of drawings for the house Solomon built for Sabetha. The drawings *looked* just right, although James would never tell anybody that he was disappointed with the way the house turned out, boxy and graceless, like a barn with too many windows. Was it possible that he still had a few things to learn about the steps between the drawing of a house and the moving in?

In August, Lawrence celebrated its third birthday as a bona fide town. Miss Malone asked everyone to bring a piece of Lawrence history to school. Jeremy Macon brought his Sharps rifle. Just about every family, except James's, of course, had one of these Beecher Bibles smuggled into Lawrence to fight uprisings with the proslavers. Jeremy's family had had the very first one in Lawrence.

Flint Morrison brought a magnifying glass that his father had ground. "My pa's the first oculist ever been here in Lawrence," he boasted. "Without my pa, nobody'd see where they were going and they'd be walking right into the river, I reckon."

James wondered what Will would have brought. Maybe the bullet that made him lose his leg in the battle that would keep Kansas Territory a free state.

He, James, took his prized sketchbook to school. Jeremy whooped over an exterior drawing of Solomon and Sabetha's house. "Whoa, don't it look just like the real thing! Hey, can you draw a pitcher of me, hunh?" Jeremy mugged for the portrait. Flint grabbed the sketchbook away from Jeremy and flipped through the pages, stopping here and there to run his magnifying glass over different parts. He seemed fascinated by the whole thing, until James thought Flint might be interested in architecture like he was. Maybe the two of them would build houses all over Douglas County. Maybe they could do it without cutting down a single tree. Houses of native limestone quarried nearby, or of cinnamon-red bricks that stacked neatly and locked tight at the corners. Houses nestled in the trees, so pert and perfect that you'd just stand there peeking through the trees and staring at those houses until night fell. Could you build a house right *around* a tree, letting it grow through the roof?

Meanwhile, the other six people in class passed their treasures around for everyone else to fuss over.

At the end of the day, James asked Flint Morrison to Sunday supper. He knew Flint had no mother to turn out a rabbit stew and a gooseberry pie like Ma did. Flint needed a friend, and so did James. A new friend wouldn't replace Will, but he could make the ache more tolerable.

Flint Morrison came to supper just twice before the fall leaves started turning, and then he sprang some big news. "Guess what, James Weaver. Me and my pa's moving to Leavenworth first of next week."

"New job for thy father, Flint?"

The boy's eyes grew soft as cotton. "New life altogether, James. My pa's getting hitched to a widow who ain't too ugly, and before long, we're gonna be rich. We done found us a pirate treasure trove!"

The first of April 1858, again by moonlight, James paced off twenty boot-lengths from the back door and began digging for the cowhide roll that held the Delaware Indian treaty. He'd resolved to dig it up and read it every year on this anniversary until— true to his solemn word—he'd unearth it for the last time and see to its delivery into the hands of the Delaware people.

He dug and dug, his chest thumping with the effort and a sudden fear that grabbed his heart as he realized the truth:

The treaty was gone. Stolen.

Chapter Fifty-Five
NEW TIME, OLD TIME

Poor squawky Firebird was banished to my room upstairs because, with all those people jammed into our parlor, he'd have a nervous breakdown and peck off half his feathers.

"So, are you and Mike a couple now?" asked Sally as she stuffed a cheesy Triscuit cracker in her mouth. It was hard to hear her over the crush of voices, but her tone of disapproval came through clearly.

Our bed-and-breakfast was so popular now that we were booked through the following football season, and all because of the Delaware treaty business. I could just imagine lining up cots end-to-end down the hall in the spring, when Mattie and Raymond came to trial.

"I mean, Ahn and I were just wondering, since you never have any time for us because you're goo-gooing over Mike."

I looked across the room at poor Mike, who was practically pinned against the mantel by Mr. Donnelly, the man from the Bureau of Indian Affairs. Mr. Donnelly was carefully avoiding Chief

Louis Ketchum, from the Delaware Tribal Council in Oklahoma. Chief Ketchum held a framed copy of the long-lost treaty, the original being safely locked away in a vault in Bartlesville.

Mr. Donnelly wore a tie bursting with pink and purple zinnias. They looked like they might pop right off the tie and suffocate him. I could see his lips rolling and flapping, overflowing with words. He could jam a whole paragraph into the normal pause between a question and an answer.

Mike kept reaching round the guy for handfuls of Spanish peanuts. I noticed a few things about Mike from this distance, too. One, his cute dimples deepened when he chewed, and he was chewing like mad to keep from choking Mr. Donnelly with his own zinnia tie. And two, Mike chewed with his mouth open. Peanut paste in the braces wasn't my idea of wildly romantic.

"We're just friends," I told Sally. "Don't worry, he's still available."

"Worry? I prefer someone of the *human* species. Anyway, I thought he liked Celina, that blond cheerleader with the skirts that barely cover her butt."

The TV station set up blinding lights. Several reporters stuck microphones in Mr. Donnelly's face, and that was Mike's exit cue. He dashed over to us. "Lock me in a cell with that guy for two days and I'd confess to poisoning my own grandmother."

Sally laughed. "You'd poison your grandmother, anyway. Where's Ahn?"

"At the courthouse with her brother Nho," I replied. "He's becoming a U.S. citizen today."

Jeep arrived with his two little brothers in tow. "They heard there was free food," he said sheepishly. Calvin and Luther headed right for the sweets table, and Jeep grabbed a peanut-butter ball as Luther sailed by him with a towering plate of chocolate goodies. Jeep jerked his head toward the man with zinnias hanging from his neck. "This is the guy who's going to solve all the Indian problems, hunh?"

"Right," Mike agreed. "If he doesn't talk them to death first. That's the Delaware chief over there, Jeep, next to his mother and Faith Cloud."

I reminded the boys, "Delaware come through the mother's line, you know."

"Weird," Jeep said.

"Male chauvinist," I hissed.

We heard Mr. Donnelly blathering on to the camera, and it reminded me of the Charlie Brown specials where the kids talk normally but all the adults drone in the background: wah-wha-wha-WHA-wah-wah.

The TV lights clicked off, and the room temperature dropped about ten degrees. The white gauzy curtains billowed in the breeze from the open windows. Then the camera and lights shifted to Chief Ketchum.

Alone in the crowd, Mr. Donnelly looked around for another victim.

"Oh no, he's coming this way!" Sally cried. We all turned our backs to the approaching Mouth, but Calvin tugged at Jeep's T-shirt. "Hey, this guy wants to talk to you." We all spun around and plastered smiles on our faces.

"Young people, I do admire your spunk," Mr. Donnelly said. "I haven't had a chance to congratulate you kids. Wha-wha-wah. Valiant work, setting things right. Blather-blather. For these Native Americans after some one hundred forty years of unmitigated injustice. Wha-wha-blah-blah. Negotiations with the Kansas descendants. Of course, they're not a *recognized* tribe, but we'll do what we can. Gwak-gwak-gwak. I'm spending an hour or two tomorrow with your friend Faith Cloud over there next to our brother, Chief Ketchum. Blooey-blooey-blah."

I tuned out about every fourth word, like somebody whose hearing aid shorts out.

"Proud and noble history. Righting the wrongs. Our brother the chief reminds me his people are rightfully called the Lenni Lenape within their own circles. We all have our own names for ourselves, isn't that so. Wha-wha-blah-blooey-gwak."

And then something caught my ear. I know, that sounds like I slammed a car door on my head, but you know what I mean. Mr. Donnelly said, "I understand James Baylor Weaver lived in this house. I saw the sign by the front door. I'm trained to observe details such as this. I do so admire his work, especially that monumental Kentucky House he designed in Washington."

"Kentucky House?" I asked.

"Why, yes. It's grand. Native stone quarried in Kentucky and carried in by barge. Diplomats from half the countries on this globe and their entire entourages stay at Kentucky House. Magnificent piece of architecture. Timeless." He pulled at the tight knot of his zinnias to free his flabby neck. "And then, this lost treaty business on top of all that talent. Quite a remarkable story turned up in our investigation. I don't suppose you young folks would care to hear it," he said, leading thirsty horses right to the trough.

Chapter Fifty-Six
1860
KANSAS TERRITORY

"Homer Biggers, thee is the kindest man I know," James said as he lifted a mug of Ma's hot cider.

Homer looked down at his feet, apparently embarrassed by James's remark.

"That's my boy," boasted Miz Pru.

"Careful thee isn't too proud," Ma cautioned, but her eyes danced.

James looked around at the whole family assembled at Solomon's house for Homer's fortieth birthday party—Sabetha and Solomon and their baby, Elizabeth; Miz Pru and Callie; Rebecca, Ma, Pa, and himself.

In another few months, James would be going back to Boston to start his studies as an architect, and he was already missing these kindly people.

He took a swallow of the cider, which burned his throat, but it was the kind of hurt that felt good.

Solomon's knee was Elizabeth's rocking horse, and the baby giggled as Solomon said, "Folks, we all know Brother Homer wouldn't be celebrating this birthday, none of us would, hadn't been for young James."

"Uh-huh. You bought our freedom, boy," Miz Pru agreed, and her words startled James because she couldn't know what had really happened. None of them knew, except Ma and Pa, the terrible price that was paid for their freedom by the Indians, and then there was Will Bowers blown to bits, and his ma grieving so, even three years later.

As usual, Callie read his thoughts. She said, "I'm awful sorry about that one-legged boy, James. He wasn't half a coward."

James nodded, remembering Will scouting on ahead with his empty leg swinging through clearings in the woods. And then he wondered if he could ever forgive himself for what he'd done to the Delaware people. He and Pa had talked to Chief Fall Leaf about the treaty, and everybody was hunting for the treaty, but the land couldn't be safely in the hands of the Delaware until it was found. "At least everyone knows it exists," Pa had reassured James. "They'll find it one day, and everything will be set right. I've offered them my legal services."

Ma had studied the situation in silent prayer for the longest time, and finally she'd told James, "Thee dealt honorably with a dishonorable man. As my father used to say—"

"A man's word is like a mountain."

"Why, yes, thee remembers!" She'd reached over and patted his arm, which was about as affectionate as Ma ever got in public. "I believe thee did the right thing, James Weaver. Thy grandfather would be proud of thee."

Her blessing had eased James considerably.

"Well, get on with the merrymaking," Miz Pru muttered. "Supper ready yet, Sabetha? Our bellies are howling, and I smell Miz Weaver's sweet potato pie clear to my bones."

"I'm setting it on the table now," Sabetha said.

As the bowls of steaming food came to the table, James raised his mug of cider again in tribute to the sweet man whose birthday they were celebrating. "Homer, I've known thee for three years now. Thee saved our skins many times. I know thee to be a good, kind human being."

Homer rolled his blue ball up and down his arm. "No, suh. *Thee* be, suh. Me, I'm jes' good with dawgs."

Chapter Fifty-Seven
HOME AT LAST

At Mr. Donnelly's tease about a *remarkable story,* Sally and Mike and Jeep and I all sprang to attention, like a bunch of jack-in-the-boxes.

"Story?" Mike asked.

"Oh, yes, it's fully documented," Mr. Donnelly continued. "Eyewitness account. Told to an Indian agent many years after the unfortunate incident occurred. But who am I talking to? You young people probably know the story better than I do." He taunted us with these bite-size nibs of information, just begging to be coaxed for more. And we were dying for more.

Mike said, "Yeah, we know the whole story." I kicked his shin, and he blurted out, "But we wouldn't mind hearing it again."

Mr. Donnelly popped a stuffed olive in his mouth and delicately spit the pimiento into his hand. "Well, it was the year James Baylor Weaver made that trip to Kentucky to bring back the runaway slaves."

I knew it! That was the last spoke in the wheel, the final connection with Miz Lizbet.

Mr. Donnelly continued, "We know it was 1857,

because that's the date on the lost treaty. Young Weaver couldn't have been more than twelve or thirteen, not even shaving yet. He and another fellow, nobody remembers his name—a boy who lost a leg in one of John Brown's raids—and a free black man named Solomon, all of them shepherded a handful of black farmhands, a family, I believe, all the way back across the Ohio River, through Indiana and Illinois, up to St. Louis, and on into Kansas. It was right there that it happened."

"WHAT DID?" we all shouted at once.

"Why, James Baylor Weaver, the selfsame famous architect, he was faced with a tough choice, a Hobson's choice, you might say, a Sophie's choice."

Not knowing who either Hobson or Sophie was, I tapped my foot impatiently.

The pimiento dropped from Mr. Donnelly's hand, and he kicked it under the table. "Who's to say any one of us wouldn't make the same decision in his shoes, which incidentally must have been worn pretty thin after all that time walking across the rugged country. This was long before turnpikes and freeways, you understand. Young folks like you can't imagine such a primitive time."

Mike prodded him. "What did James Weaver *do*, Mr. Donnelly?"

"The choice, yes. It was either the runaways or the Delaware. He had to sell out one for the other. An eyewitness saw it all. Well, that's what an eyewitness is, isn't it, someone who sees things?"

"Saw what?" I asked.

"Saw that boy, Weaver, accept the unratified treaty, which he agreed to hide for a time, in exchange for money to free those black people from the hands of a greedy slave catcher who would have sent them back to Kentucky. Well, by George, I guess that's why he named that stately building Kentucky House. I never put those two together before."

"Mr. Donnelly!" Sally cried.

"I digress. Yes, well. The eyewitness was one of the runaways, believe it or not, who came forward and told the story to an itinerant preacher, an unimpeachable source, I'll have you know. This was some ten or fifteen years after the fact. Well, by then nobody knew where the document was, and no one could quite remember what the terms were for sure, and, well, that's how Indian affairs sometimes come to ruin. But we're making reparations today, you can rest assured. Although they're not a *recognized* tribe, you understand. But we'll do what we can."

Jeep said, "I wonder who it was who told the story."

"I've got the name right here in my notes." Mr. Donnelly pulled a small spiral notebook out of his inside pocket and flipped through a few pages. "Ah, here it is. A man by the name of Biggers. Homer Biggers."

Jeep's brothers had been listening to the whole conversation, and now Luther said, "Hey, Calvin, who's bigger, Mrs. Bigger or Mrs. Bigger's baby?"

Calvin pushed a mush of cookies to the side of his mouth like a wad of tobacco and answered, "Mrs. Bigger's baby. He's just a *little* Bigger." Luther and Calvin high-fived each other, then Luther said, "Me and Calvin always tell that joke, because we've got Biggerses in our family."

Jeep nodded, holding on to a floor lamp like it was a post in a speeding bus. He looked pale enough to faint. "Momma always talks about a Callie Biggers, about how she was the first black woman doctor in Kansas."

I raised a cup of slushy cranberry punch in a toast to all those amazing people who lived before microwaves and E-mail and sticky-notes and Caller ID. "To Dr. Callie Biggers."

"To James Baylor Weaver," Mr. Donnelly said, waving another green olive. "An American treasure, sure enough."

And to Miz Lizbet, I added silently. Finally her bones could stop rattling in my brain.

Somehow I knew there was still more I had to settle—somebody else's bones, but I didn't know whose.

Chapter Fifty-Eight
February 1861
STATE OF KANSAS

James had been set to leave for Boston right after the winter thaw, but war was a fiery glow on the horizon.

"Best go today, son," Pa warned. "This land will be riddled with bullets too soon, too soon."

"Caleb Weaver!" Ma scolded him even as she packed the picnic hamper for James to take on his travels.

"Mrs. Weaver, thee mustn't bury thy fair head in the sand. Kansas is a state now, but at the same time, seven of her older sisters have pulled out of the Union. War, mark my words."

Ma furiously stuffed two loaves of bread into the hamper, along with a flour sack full of dried apples and sunflower seeds and a basket of fried chicken and half a dozen molasses cookies.

James snapped the lock on his trunk. There was nothing else to do but leave. Sliding the trunk toward the door, he was reminded of that basket in Kentucky and hauling it upstairs loaded with hay and stones, and downstairs loaded with Callie.

How close they'd come to being discovered! But that was nearly four years ago, and now Solomon and Miz Lizbet's family was safe in the brand-new State of Kansas.

Buttoning the coat of his first grown-up suit, he wondered how he could bring himself to say good-bye to these people he'd been among all his life.

Rebecca, grown shapely overnight, hung back shyly. When she thought he wasn't looking, she poked some trinket into the hamper. It was a surprise he'd save for the lonely, icy-track train ride to Boston.

Ma handed James a Bible. The soft, worn leather and flaking gold leaf made his throat tight with longing for his family before he was even out the door.

Pa tried to ease up the solemn mood. "A Bible, Millicent? Does thee think the boy needs a thick pillow on his journey?"

Ma snapped back, "Thee might rest thy *own* world-weary eyes on such a pillow, Caleb."

And then they all heard the *clop-clop* of a horse out front—Solomon come to drive James to Kansas City.

Ma wound a red wool muffler around James's neck and hung the picnic hamper over his arm. "We shall be watching the mail, son," she said, then turned away before her tears embarrassed them both.

Pa and Rebecca walked him to the coach. "Morning, Solomon," Pa said. Solomon nodded, but James noticed him trying to be invisible through these impossible good-byes. It stabbed his heart to realize that Solomon's would be the last face he'd see as he boarded the train.

Rebecca clung to him like moss to a rock. Three years earlier he'd have pried her off and chased her back into the house. "Thee's the best brother," she stammered through her tears.

"There's not been much competition, Rebecca," James said, forcing a smile.

"Daughter, go on in. It's way below freezing."

Reluctantly, she waved all the way into the house, and in a minute, James saw her in the window, waving still.

Pa said, "Thee's seventeen now, James, a man off to learn his trade."

He didn't *feel* like a man right now.

Pa hoisted the trunk up into the coach. Puffing warm clouds into the frigid air, Pa said, "Thy mother is a woman of few words—"

"Few words, Pa?" What a relief when they both laughed.

"Well, few *gentling* words. But I've known this woman the better part of two decades, and I believe I know her heart. Thy mother and I, we're both immensely proud of thee, son. We look for great things from thee in the years ahead."

Beautiful buildings, James thought, monuments to the good, peace-loving family who'd brought him up and now generously sent him away to his future.

Then Pa half hugged him and half shook his hand, and James climbed up into the coach. "Take care of my boy, Solomon."

"Yes, sir, I always have," Solomon replied, "except when he was taking care of me and mine."

The mare shifted from foot to foot to keep warm. Pa gently slapped her rear and turned back to James. "Come home to us with a good woman, son. That would please thy mother."

"One just like Ma?" James teased.

"Well, a mite less stubborn, I reckon. Godspeed, son."

Chapter Fifty-Nine
WHO KNOWS?

Here in Kansas, our summers sizzle, and we get out of school before Memorial Day. The official reason is that lots of kids have to work the family farm, but I live in a city, and I've never met a single farmer. I think the real reason is that nobody wants to pay to air-condition the schools.

Anyway, by the middle of June, summer's already peeking over the fence between *Wow, school's out!* and *Phew, I'm bored*. One hot, sticky Sunday in June, my parents proposed their deadly cure-all for boredom, the Family Outing.

"Wonderful idea, Jeffrey! Where to?"

Dad was reading the What's Doing? section of the newspaper. "Hey, this looks good. Council Grove's having their annual Wah-shun-gah Days."

"Wah who?" I asked. I was definitely *not* going, no matter what they bribed me with.

Dad picked tantalizing details out of the paper. "Festival, parade, rafting, Indian powwow."

"Not interested." I had control of the remote, and I was scrolling through the sound bites of fifty-three channels.

"You can bring a friend," Mom said. She was already setting tea out on the porch to brew in the sun and was dragging Genoa salami and provolone out of the fridge for sandwiches. A Family Outing required a picnic and ants and mosquitoes and salami sandwiches. "How about Ahn, or Sally?"

I hit on an old Mary Tyler Moore rerun—"Oh, Mr. Gr-a-a-ant!"—and flew past it to land on a black-and-white sci-fi movie featuring a hokey monster with bugging eyes and tentacles way out of control. That reminded me of Mike. "Can I bring Mike?"

"A *boy*?"

"You were a boy once, Dad."

"I know, that's what worries me."

"Oh, Jeffrey, they're just friends. Sure, honey, ask Mike."

Council Grove is this little town about a hundred miles from Lawrence. It used to be a way station along the Santa Fe Trail. A bunch of Indians signed a treaty with the U.S. government to make it safe for whites to travel along the trail. Was I *never* going to be free of old Indian treaties? But I agreed to go. And that's how Mike and I had our second nondate, which practically meant we were engaged.

The town was swarming with people walking and dragging babies in wagons, and dogs trotting down the center of the street like they owned the town. I'm sure all two thousand residents were out for

Wah-shun-gah Days, plus about twenty thousand of their closest friends.

Mike and I ditched Mom and Dad for a couple of hours and went exploring on our own. Across the street was a sign over a building:

HAYS HOUSE 1857

I said, "Hey, isn't that the date on the treaty James Weaver buried?"

We bounded across the street to read the small print: OLDEST CONTINUOUS RESTAURANT WEST OF THE MISSISSIPPI.

Mike, who was definitely sick of hearing about James Weaver, said, "Bet they've got fossilized food left over from 1857. Your boyfriend James probably had a prairie dog steak here, and they saved the bones in a glass case. Let's go over to the parade."

We elbowed our way through the three-deep crowd. The 4-H float passed in front of us now, with kids our age trying to keep actual goats and sheep from leaping off the float. A battalion of kiddie majorettes in embarrassing semimilitary uniforms occasionally caught the batons they tossed toward the clear blue sky.

"Check out the fifties Cadillac!" Mike shouted. Shriners in weird little hats that looked like upside-down sand pails sat in the convertible zooming down Main Street at speeds exceeding two miles per hour.

"Ladies and gentlemen!" a huge voice boomed out at us from speakers up and down the street. "Presenting Suzanne Yaeger, our newly crowned Miss Kansas!" The big-haired queen sat in the back of the Caddy in a hot pink strapless gown. She did the Queen Elizabeth wave Faith Cloud talked about and flashed her orthodontist's handiwork. Mike, of course, was panting like a dog.

I swear, it wasn't just an effort to distract him, but that's when I noticed the building across the street that definitely didn't fit with this town. It was two big stories of red brick, with stone trim, little turrety things, and a dome and Roman arches. It looked like half the ancient world had been cobbled right here in downtown Council Grove, Kansas. I yanked Mike across the street, tearing in front of the high school band in its brassy rendition of "Hello, Dolly."

The building was called the Farmers and Drovers Bank. Mike proclaimed it "ug-LEE," and "even worse up close than from across the street."

"No, I think it's gorgeous. Who would build such a thing in a dinky town like this, Mike?" I studied the cornerstone: built in 1892.

"You don't suppose—"

Mike and I said it at the same time: "James Weaver!"

We walked all around the building and couldn't

298

find the architect's name. It could have been built by Popeye or Steven Spielberg, for all we knew, but I was convinced that it was James's work. I snapped pictures from every angle for Ahn and Sally and Jeep. I ran across the intersection and climbed onto the hood of a truck to capture the second-floor arches. Inside, someone was working right through the parade, her face green in the glow of her computer.

A computer in one of James Weaver's buildings? Wouldn't he go nuts seeing all that had happened in the century and a half since he'd moved to Kansas Territory?

From the blaring speakers we heard, "Folks, let's welcome the junior senator from the great State of Kansas, Senator Rhain Buth!" The crowd went berserk, and I craned my neck to get a peek at the handsome young senator.

Mike yanked me down from the truck, saying, "Let's go. I hate crowds."

"Where to?" I shouted.

He patted the Council Grove brochure flapping out of his back pocket. "Worlds to conquer," he said.

Mike bought a Pepsi from a street vendor and asked for two straws. Some kid's cotton candy glopped into my hair as we ripped a hole in the crowd to explore quieter corners of Council Grove. I kept glancing back at the Farmers and Drovers Bank, wondering, wondering, while I peeled pink sticky stuff out of my hair and wiped it down the back of Mike's T-shirt.

The crowd was just a quiet roar in the distance when we came to the Monument to the Unknown Indian. Mike walked right past it, but I tugged at the back of his shirt and made him stop.

For some reason, the statue sent chills through me, despite the 98-degree day. What kind of Indian was this? Kaw? Kiowa? Pawnee? Osage? Probably one of those tribes. Delaware? Probably not; there'd been so few of them.

I moved away from Mike, needing space. The sun beat down on my back. I could already feel my neck and shoulders turning lobster red, and new freckles popping out on my nose. Then a cloud slid past the sun, turning the ground under the monument a cool gray. It was all the time I needed, just long enough to convince myself that I knew who this Indian was.

Mike rattled ice in our empty Pepsi cup. "He looks like the guy on those red Big Chief tablets we had in second grade." Mike looked up into the bronze face of the statue, whose gaze was fixed across the huge prairie. "What do you see out there, Big Chief Anonymous?" He leaned against the base of the statue with his arms folded across his chest, grinning. The sun glinted off his braces. Two more years, and he'd have teeth just like Miss Kansas. "Cute guy, whoever he is. Not that I like guys."

"I know who he is," I said quietly.

"Yeah? Who?"

I shook my head. He'd think I was a lunatic if I told him the Indian's name was Samuel Straightfeather.

Mike circled the monument. "It doesn't say the guy's name anywhere, just like it didn't say the architect's name over at that ugly bank. You're hallucinating again, Dana. Too much sun."

But it all fit together—James Weaver and his astonishing building, which looked like nothing else in town, and Council Grove, where lots of Indian treaties were signed, and now this haunting statue.

The building was James's, but maybe not.

The statue was of Samuel Straightfeather, but maybe not.

It didn't matter anymore.

The sun shimmered on the dry ground beneath the statue, almost like a rippling patch of water. Mike was impatient to get moving. He said, "Forget it. Nobody knows who this guy is supposed to be. He's *unknown*, right? That's the whole point. Use your noggin, Dana."

He's Samuel Straightfeather.

"Hey, take my picture," Mike said.

Great-great-too-many-greats-grandfather of Faith Cloud.

Just as I had at high noon, on the day of Bo Prairie Fire's funeral, I silently asked, *What year is it,*

Mr. Prairie Fire? And I heard the old Indian's raspy voice sputtering between coughing fits, "Why, it's *this* year, girlie, eighteen and fifty-seven."

Mike was saying, "Heads up, Dana. Hit the red button. I can't stand here looking cute much longer." *Click.* "When the picture comes back, we'll call it Photo of the Unknown White Kid with the Unknown Indian."

Unknown to everyone, but me.